John Singleton Copley

JOHN SINGLETON COPLEY: *The Three Princesses*

Royal Collection

John Singleton
Copley

JAMES THOMAS FLEXNER

FORDHAM UNIVERSITY PRESS
NEW YORK
1993

LC 93-3349

ISBN 0-8232-1523-7

This volume is a completely revised and greatly enlarged version of the biography of John Singleton Copley originally published by The Viking Press, Inc., in 1939 as part of James Thomas Flexner's book *America's Old Masters*.

First edition published by Houghton Mifflin Company, 1948

Second edition, Fordham University Press, 1993

Library of Congress Cataloging-in-Publication Data

Flexner, James Thomas, 1908–
John Singleton Copley / by James Thomas Flexner.
p. cm.
Originally published: Boston : Houghton Mifflin, 1948.
Includes bibliographical references and index.
ISBN 0-8232-1523-7
1. Copley, John Singleton, 1738–1815.
2. Painters—United States—
Biography. I. Title.
ND237.C7F6   1993
759.13—dc20
[B]   93-3349
CIP

Printed in the United States of America

To my grandson,
HARRY FLEXNER DESMOND

Foreword

ALTHOUGH no schoolboy learns the date by rote, 1738 was an important year in the development of the New World. It marked the birth of America's first major creator in any branch of the arts. Literature, sculpture, architecture, music had to wait several generations before any of them produced a figure commensurate with the painter, John Singleton Copley.

Copley lived two lives and had a career to go with each. Growing up in provincial Boston, he became a professional painter while yet in his teens, and before he had reached twenty-one he achieved a miracle: he painted greater pictures than any he had ever known. Having left behind him all signboards, all beacons, all blazes on the trees, he was forced to penetrate the age-old wilderness of art by reckonings made from the stars of his own genius. The path he took was of his own hewing, as native to the Colonies as the territory through which it passed. Copley's portraits were the first profound esthetic expression of the American spirit. They made forever manifest the personalities and the faces of the Americans who first in war and then in peaceful negotiation created the United States.

When he was thirty-six, he left the New World and his old life behind him; he sailed for the fabled art galleries of Europe. A self-taught artist who had already painted great pictures, he saw all at once, in a wild phantasmagoria of styles and colors, the works of Raphael and Reynolds, Van Dyck, Rubens, Poussin, and hundreds more. Antique statues burst upon his consciousness: Venus and Apollo stood in naked splendor before the man who had rarely seen a nude work of art; Laocoön writhed and Niobe wept for her children. Copley was dazzled and exalted and bewildered. Then there was the necessity of coming to earth again, of painting again now that he had seen great art. Could he keep the virtues he had worked out for himself in the quiet of provincial cities; could a mature painter graft on to a homemade style the wonder and burden of centuries?

His trip through the Continent over, Copley embarked in London on his second career. And amazingly, instead of repeating by rote the shiny new tricks he had acquired, he became as great an innovator in the mature European tradition as he had been in the adolescent American. While Doctor Johnson still dictated English taste, while Wordsworth and Coleridge were still little boys, Copley painted pictures that presage the Romantic movement. His canvases depict wild, bloody action in strange places, and also the dramas of contemporary heroes at home. Quickening a generation later in France, his influence helped mold such artists as Géricault and Delacroix.

We shall here be as much concerned with Copley the man as Copley the painter; indeed to separate the two would be as delicate an operation as cutting a human being in half. The Boston and the London in which he lived will be major characters in our history. There is a success story to tell—a trip from poverty to affluence, from obscurity to fame—but more basic will be our attempt to comprehend the development of a profound and brilliant mind. Copley's life flared up into political action only once, on the occasion when single-handed he tried to head off the American Revolution by bringing the Whigs and Tories together in a compromise that would have made unnecessary the Boston Tea Party. For the rest, he was dedicated to his art. His brain was like a sensitive instrument that flies a powerful airplane through weather that has grounded lesser craft. We shall watch the movements of the dials and interpret them, as best we may, in relation to the mechanism within. Then before our horrified eyes the plane will veer from its course and crash against the mountains of an alien land.

Contents

[xi]

List of Illustrations

* *Illustrations follow page 126*

[xiii]

John Singleton Copley

ONE

Terror on Long Wharf

THE PICTURE stood against the wall of Sir Joshua Reynolds's London studio, striking a strange note in that center of mid-eighteenth-century elegance. The great English painter scowled at it in amazement, for, as he later explained, he had never seen a canvas that gave him quite the same feeling. This portrait of a young boy was a strange mixture of the modern and the old-fashioned, the sophisticated and the crude. The looped red curtain in the background was a stock stage-set borrowed from the imitators of Sir Peter Lely, the school Sir Joshua himself had overthrown, but the pose of the youngster before it was startlingly up to date. He did not stand nobly in one of the stylized positions decreed by aristocratic convention. Interrupted by the artist in his play with a winged squirrel, he glanced up naturally as if to see who had come into the room. Reynolds, bending close to the canvas, observed that the outlines were drawn with the most exquisite accuracy, but that they had been filled in with color in a manner that was unsophisticated, almost crude. Then he stepped back from the pic-

[1]

ture and realized once more that, for all its awkwardness, it struck the sensibilities with the power of a cannonball.

Sir Joshua turned to Lord Buchan, who had brought the picture into his studio, and asked the painter's name. Shrugging, the connoisseur replied that he could not remember; it was a name he had never heard before. The canvas had been left with him by an American sea captain he had met somewhere, so he assumed it was by an American. Indeed, he was sure of only one thing; the painter, whoever he was, wished to have the picture exhibited at the Society of Artists, then the leading artistic organization in England.

Sir Joshua could hardly believe that so fine a picture could have been done by an unknown Colonial. Eager to unravel the mystery, he called in Benjamin West, an American-born painter who enjoyed great celebrity in London. West turned the picture on its back and stared at the frame on which the canvas was stretched. "That's American pine wood," he said. The picture was certainly by an American, but by what American? None of the Colonials in England painted in that style or so well. Ecstatically West praised the "delicious color worthy of Titian," and although Sir Joshua, who thought the coloring cold, winced at this, he agreed that the picture was excellent, more than good enough to exhibit at the Society of Artists. However, there was a rule against showing anonymous pictures; the name of the painter must be discovered, and that at once.

West rushed out and questioned Joseph Wright, a young compatriot who had, in West's words, "just made his appearance in the art in a surprising degree of merit." But Wright denied that he had painted the picture. From then on, West and Reynolds scratched their heads in vain; they could think of nobody. Finally Reynolds was forced to send the canvas, although its painter was still unidentified, to the exhibition with his own pictures. He argued that the portrait was so outstanding, it should be hung despite the rule against anonymous pictures, and the conservative academicians, after poring one by one over the strange canvas, agreed that an exception would have to be made for so remarkable a work of art.

However, before the exhibition opened, Lord Buchan hurried to Sir Joshua's studio, followed by a large, seafaring American. Captain Bruce seemed out of place in the elegant chamber where hung many portraits of stylish ladies, but it was he who had brought the painting to Lord Buchan. It was done, he said, by a young Bostonian named Copley, John Singleton Copley. Sir Joshua looked at Bruce with increasing amazement as the sea captain told him that Copley, although twenty-eight years old, had never been out of the provincial city of Boston, and had never in his life seen a picture worthy to be called a painting. Bruce was to write home to Copley what Reynolds had said to him: "Considering the disadvantages you had labored under, it is a very wonderful performance. . . . He did not know one painter at home, who had all the advantages that Europe could give them, that could equal it, and that if you are capable of producing such a piece by the mere efforts of your own genius, with the advantages of example and instruction which you could have in Europe, you would be a valuable acquisition to the art and one of the first painters in the world." In fact, Reynolds was so excited that he forgot to write down the name of the painter. Thus it came about that the first picture by John Singleton Copley to be publicly exhibited anywhere in the world was mislabeled: the artist's name was given as "William Copley."

The romantic story of the masterpiece that had emerged unheralded from the wilderness soon spread through the compact art world of London. Connoisseurs flocked to see the picture of a provincial child leaning intently over a table while his pet flying squirrel nibbled at a nut. Soon the name of Copley was on every cultivated tongue. On the strength of this one picture, the unknown and misnamed painter was given the highest honor the English art world could offer: he was elected a member of the Society of Artists. People wondered how such a genius could have sprung up spontaneously under the shadow of America's primeval trees.

The best evidence that exists, which is not entirely conclusive, indicates that John Singleton Copley was born in or near Boston on July 3, 1738. According to family tradition, his parents, who were of English stock, had arrived from Ireland at about that time, and his father had sailed on to the West Indies, where he died shortly after the boy was born. Copley's early years are shrouded in mystery, for the inhabitants of Boston, with whom the searching of genealogical records is almost a mania, have been unable to find any mention of his birth or baptism.

A newspaper advertisement, however, shows that before Copley was ten his mother was living over a tobacco shop she operated on Long Wharf. Boston was at that time the largest city of British America and the most important commercial center. Since the old harbor, most of which is now filled in with land, was very shallow, the end of State Street had been extended some two thousand feet out into the bay to form a pier so broad that houses could be built on one side. In one of these Copley spent his early childhood. Looking from the back windows he saw water lapping the foundation of his dwelling, and from the front windows he had a view that seemed calculated to make any boy's heart swell with the romance of travel and far places. Separated from his house by only a fifteen-foot walk lay moored the square-rigged boats that brought Boston its prosperity; sometimes twenty or more were tied to the long quay. The day and the night as well were loud with the creaking of blocks as square sails blossomed from high spars.

Daily the boats came to and fro; daily the future painter watched ships emerge tiny from between the outlying islands and grow momentarily larger until the wild cormorant of the ocean lay bobbing at rest by his front door. He watched the sailors stand in a dizzy line on the rigging as they lashed down the furled sails, and then his mother's tobacco shop would be full of the sounds of voices. Standing behind the counter, answering with alacrity demands for tobacco "cut, pigtail, or spun," the boy served mariners who had returned from the seven seas.

Excitement flared as the endless war with Spain unrolled. Privateers set out from Long Wharf with the blessings of the Commonwealth, half-hidden guns peeping black from portholes. The sailors who crowded into Mrs. Copley's shop for a last hunk of tobacco before the adventure began had cutlasses in their belts, and their voices were thin with anticipation. Watching warlike sails vanish down the horizon, an imaginative lad could coin endless visions of blood and glory. Then months later there would be a running of feet on Long Wharf and a staring from the tip as the privateer came home towing a prize.

In 1748, when Copley was ten, the frigate *Bethel* out of Boston, armed with only fourteen guns and carrying only thirty-eight men, brought following docilely in its wake a Spanish treasure ship of twenty-four guns. More than a hundred prisoners lay bound beneath its decks. The breathless rumor went round that in the Spaniard's hold was a hundred thousand pounds in ducats and doubloons.

We should expect an adventurous boy brought up in such an atmosphere to run off to sea at an early age, ship as a cabin boy, and return at last resplendent with strange oaths and cutlass wounds. Or, if he became a painter, we should expect his canvases to be instinct with the joy of adventure: battles would be glorified, generals and privateers. But we may search Copley's work in vain for such pictures as these. Neither interested nor impressed by men of physical action, Copley idealized sensitive intellectual faces, portraying them so lovingly that they formed the subject matter of his finest portraits. And when in the manner of his time he turned to scenes of war, his canvases revealed no taste for carnage. In the best of his battle pictures, *The Death of Major Pierson* (Plates 6 and 26), the eye is caught and held by a weeping group in the foreground; the wife and child of the dying hero wail, louder than the guns and the shouts of victory, their anguish at man's inhumanity to man.

Copley's few paintings of the sea are tinged with horror. In his *The Repulse of the Floating Batteries at Gibraltar*, he shows the ocean full of the writhing forms of dying men; half-naked, mangled bodies struggle in every contortion of pain with the enveloping flood. Only one other of his important canvases deals primarily with the ocean, and that is a brilliantly painted representation of nightmare. In the foreground a naked and defenseless swimmer sprawls in a contortion of anguish; he is being attacked by a shark. Behind him several men in a small boat gesture to bring assistance when assistance seems past hope. And the water in which the victim flounders is a sickly yellow-green, a stringy and repulsive element in which naked men are attacked by monsters. (Plate 8.)

Whenever, in the many letters that have come down to us, Copley refers to ships or the sea, he does so with displeasure. If he had to travel from Boston to New York and Philadelphia, he traveled by land, although the roads were so bad that water offered a much quicker and more comfortable route. As we shall see, Copley hesitated for years before he made the trip across the ocean so necessary to a Colonial painter, and he could never force himself to return.

Eighteenth-century seafaring was not altogether romantic; there was another side that might affect a lad more sensitive than adventuresome. Impressed seamen who had been knocked down in the streets of London and carried off in stinking holds without a word to their families; battered, wincing derelicts limping into Mrs. Copley's shop, their hands trembling when they picked up the tobacco the boy dealt out to them. In 1747, Commodore Charles Knowles tried this British custom in Boston. Annoyed by desertions, he landed a press gang that kidnaped apprentices as they strolled down Long Wharf. Then the Boston populace rose and rioted for three long days, while the royal governor fled to Castle William and the naval commander threatened to bombard the town. With anxious eyes, the nine-year-old Copley watched sails rise on the British frigate as it maneuvered into position. But the commodore did not shoot, and in the end was forced to release the men he had stolen.

Flanking Mrs. Copley's shop on Long Wharf were grogshops which made the night hideous with the sound of drunken singing and drunken fights. We need not be surprised that Copley reacted violently against his childhood environment. Induced by his own children to talk of those unhappy days, he told them that he had escaped from brutal reality into the recesses of his own mind; he became a quiet and studious lad. When the tough waterfront boys, seeing his pale face at the window, dared him to come out and hooted him as a sissy, he fled to an empty room, where he comforted himself by drawing pictures on the walls. Family tradition tells us that at seven or eight, he sketched in charcoal a group of martial figures engaged in some unnamed adventure. The Bible also was a source of inspiration to the well-brought-up lad, who showed his literal-mindedness by painting the sea Moses crossed a glowing red. Or did he think of all oceans as tinged with blood?

Copley's letters reveal that he had been well educated. Probably he went to the school conducted by Peter Pelham, for during 1748 his mother married that estimable widower. A month later, the following advertisement appeared in the Boston *Gazette*: "Mrs. Mary Pelham (formerly the widow Copley, on the Long Wharf, tobacconist) is removed to Lindel's Row, against the Quakers' Meeting House, near the upper end of King Street, Boston, where she continues to sell the best Virginia tobacco, cut, pigtail, and spun, of all sorts, by wholesale and retail at the cheapest prices."

Thus Copley escaped from the waterfront. However, his mother's marriage had an even more important consequence; Peter Pelham was the first well-trained mezzotint-scraper to appear in the Colonies. He had already earned an English reputation before coming to America about 1725, and on his arrival he immediately secured all the business there was for engravings after portraits of leading citizens. Yet all the business there was did not suffice to keep him in food and lodgings; he was forced to open a school, where, according to an advertisement published the year of Copley's birth, "young gentlemen and ladies may be taught dancing, writing, reading, painting, and needlework." His dancing assemblies were immediately criticized by the pious burghers of Boston. "What could give encouragement to so licentious and expensive a diversion in a town famous for its decency and good order? . . ." an indignant citizen asked in the Boston *Gazette*. "When we look back upon the transactions of our forefathers and read the wonderful story of their godly zeal, their pious resolution, and their public virtues, how should we blush and lament our present corruption of manners and decay of religious and civil discipline. . . . In vain will our ministers preach charity, moderation, and humility to an audience whose thoughts are engaged in scenes of splendor and magnificence, and whose time and money are consumed in dress and dancing."

Blue laws hampered the artistic-minded of Boston at every turn. During Copley's thirteenth year, the town had the excitement of its first theatrical performance. When two English actors announced that they would present *An Orphan, or Unhappy Marriage* at the British Coffee House and persuaded some rash Bostonians to take the minor rôles, the citizens were so shocked at the idea of a play that everyone wanted to see it. A huge crowd gathered outside the coffee house, on King Street near Copley's home, and finding that there was not room to admit them all, they rioted. Immediately, with the entire approval of the mob that had been so eager to get in, the government passed an "Act to Prevent Stage Plays and Other Theatrical Entertainments," on the grounds that they "occasioned unnecessary expenses, discouraged industry," and increased "immorality, impiety, and contempt for religion." This law was re-enacted as late as 1784.

Perhaps because of religious opposition, all Pelham's innumerable activities did not bring in enough money to enable his new wife to give up her tobacco shop; the house to which Copley moved was continually alive with the voices of customers and the droning of pupils. However, it contained a marvelous room into which the boy could flee. Here was the scarred table on which Pelham made his prints, here were all the sharp and intricate tools of art. His stepfather took delight in teaching the eager youngster how to engrave. Pelham occasionally did oil paintings too, and he allowed the boy to dabble in bright pigments, to spread paint with soft, imported brushes. Or, first making sure Copley's hands were clean, Pelham would bring down from a shelf the prints of English paintings that he tried to sell the parsimonious Colonial connoisseurs; Copley fingered in excitement black-and-white representations of portraits by Highmore and Hudson, and wondered whether a mere American could ever do as well. Indeed, chance had thrown the lad into one of the few households in the Colonies that had direct contact with European art.

Painting in America goes back to the very beginnings of our history, but always it was conducted on what we should today consider an artisan basis. The workmen came from the humbler classes, for gentlemen, although willing to dabble a little in an amateurish way, regarded a serious interest in art as be-

neath their social station. After Governor Gooch of Virginia
had been induced to lend his coach to an artist, he complained
that "it looks a little odd for a governor to show so much favor
to a painter."

A typical early American limner was at an early age apprenticed to a trade: clockmaking, or saddling, or, if he were very
lucky, house and sign painting. After reaching his majority,
and setting out for himself, he followed the natural pattern of
artisans in a society where the demand for skilled labor exceeded the supply; he added new occupations to his stock in
trade, becoming proficient in a half-dozen specialties. If he had
an interest in design and could procure the necessary colors, he
would paint, at first perhaps for his own amusement. When
people offered to pay him for portraits and decorative pictures,
he would go into that business too, and, if he were successful
enough, art would grow to overshadow his other crafts.

Although our early workmen created every kind of picture
they could think of, or which they read about in books, portraits
offered the best possibilities for profits and were likely to be
more esthetically successful than other modes. Subject paintings ran up against many difficulties. Genre never became ac-
climated, perhaps because American society was evolving too
fast to permit the development of static social symbols. To depict scenes from the antique was, of course, considered very
knowing, but it was hard for a Colonial to paint with conviction
such subjects as *The Judgement of Hercules*. The imaginations
of the painters were peopled not with sibyls but with seraphim;
Jehovah ruled, Satan fought, and the angels choired to the stars.
Had the Colonials been permitted to depict religious subjects
wholeheartedly, they might well have produced deeply felt

pictures, but when an artist drew a scene from the Bible, he knew he was wallowing deep in sin. The Protestants objected to religious art.

Landscape painting, too, suffered from doctrinal difficulties. The early American God was the vengeful God of the Old Testament. He did not express himself through nature, but stood back and judged nature, usually to its disadvantage. This hostile attitude toward field and forest had a particular aptness to the pioneers, for the wilderness was far from a charming companion; life could be wrested from nature only by vicious toil. Landscape painting reached no glories until nature became tamer and the old theology gave way to a gentle mist of pantheism that softened the rocks and brought out the golden shimmer in the trees.

The Puritan philosophy, which frowned on display and placed its emphasis on useful things, was perfectly suited to a civilization that lay uneasily between a tempestuous sea and an even more tempestuous wilderness. Houses had to be built somehow and furnished with necessities, land had to be tilled quickly before people starved, guns had to be forever primed to withstand savage invasions. Nor, as the settlement advanced, did this situation basically change. True, cities took the place of villages, but they brought with them new problems of organization, and always in the back country there was more land to be developed and fought for. In addition, the system of quit-rents, and the British laws which limited American manufactures and gave England advantages in commerce, kept Americans continually in debt to the mother country. Although some Colonial merchants and planters became rich and purse-proud, they were never as firmly in the saddle as their counterparts in

England. One could see fine houses, and jewels, and ruffles of rare lace, but American luxury was a pale reflection of luxury as it existed in the Old World. There was much less superflux to spend on art.

One aspect of painting, however, was useful, practical, and perfectly in accord with Puritan thinking which increasingly emphasized the importance of the individual. Powerful divines and rising merchants could not endure the thought that posterity would never see their features. In the absence of photography, they had to patronize painters, as did the settlers who wished to send their "effigies" back to families left in another Colony or across the water. All through the Colonial period, there was a steady demand for portraits.

Likenesses were turned out in thousands by hundreds of painters. According to the traditional standards of European art, the pictures were without exception crude. No record demonstrates that before Copley's generation any American-born painter crossed the ocean to the galleries of the Old World. Ignorant of great art, the native limners did their best work when most completely self-inspired. During the nineteenth century, it is true, Americans blushed with embarrassment at the roughness of our early portraits, and often commissioned restorers to repaint an ancestor into more acceptable shape. But today we find great virtues in America's first pictures. Indeed, we prefer them to some of the sophisticated European confections which the Colonial artists read about and would have gleefully imitated had they been enabled to do so.

For the American portraits, although simply conceived and flatly painted, carry with them the freshness of unspoiled vision. When fate entered the shop of a naturally gifted Colonial artisan and placed a paint brush in the hand that had just put down a saw or saddler's tool, she inspired an agile mind to struggle on its own with the eternal problems of art. Unable to remember how Raphael had lighted a hand, how Lely had folded drapery, the artist had to work these things out for himself. If he achieved a solution, it was profoundly felt, deeply his own.

Occasionally, the early American painters were joined by artists from abroad. These imports were usually very simple craftsmen whose names were unknown to the great practitioners of the European courts; they brought with them provincial styles almost as crude as the work of their American contemporaries. The great exception to this rule was John Smibert, the artist who was to play so important a rôle in Copley's development.

A Scot by birth, Smibert began his career humbly enough as an apprentice to an Edinburgh house painter and plasterer, but as soon as he was released from his indentures he journeyed to London, where he struggled to overcome his lack of social position and his lack of training, to become a portrait painter. Finally, fortune presented him with a three-years' trip to Italy. Being able to boast of foreign study, he became on his return a successful portraitist; not one of the most fashionable, perhaps, but yet a man of reputation. The connoisseurs were amazed when he gave up his hard-earned position to join the radical philosopher, Dean Berkeley, in a mad scheme to found in Bermuda a college for the education of the Indians. During 1728, ten years before Copley was born, Smibert accompanied Berkeley's crew of idealists to Newport. There they waited for promised funds that never came.

When the scheme finally collapsed, Smibert settled in Boston, where he made a rich marriage and secured a virtual monopoly of the best portrait commissions. A friend and business associate of Pelham, he probably gave Copley some instruction. We know the boy saw hanging in his studio the copies he had made of European masterpieces, including the one of Van Dyck's *Cardinal Bentivoglio* that was by itself to constitute the first American art school. Copley, Washington Allston, and John Trumbull, three of America's leading painters, all found in this one picture their first hints of a richer portrait style.

We can visualize Copley, not yet in his teens, bent with aching attention over the copies that brought him a pale reflection of great art. Twenty-five years later, when he was himself a famous artist, he was to see originals and write that Smibert's copies were inaccurate, miscolored, and badly drawn. But as a boy he was deeply impressed. There in the studio of a disgruntled English painter of medium ability, the muses first whispered in the ears of the Colonial genius who had never seen a really sophisticated picture.

However, Copley's period of instruction under Pelham and Smibert was short, for they both died in 1751. Pelham's estate was so small that his widow did not trouble to file an inventory; and there was another mouth in the family to feed, for Copley had a half-brother, Henry Pelham. Again poverty faced the boy who had suffered the horrors of Long Wharf. At thirteen he was forced to try to make money at the trade for which he was being trained. He set up as a painter and engraver.

TWO

Foreign Grace and Native Vigor

THE BOSTON into whose troubled waters Copley was now thrown, to sink or swim as he might, was already agitated by forces that in a quarter-century were to explode into civil war. To a casual view, however, the streets seemed tranquil enough. An Englishman might imagine himself in some provincial city of his homeland: Glasgow, perhaps, or Bristol. The wilderness, with its skyscraping trees, was miles away; the city streets ended in well-traveled lanes beyond whose hedges were neat farms. Indians were so much a rarity that everyone turned to stare.

On the surface, at least, the passers-by fell easily into the social stereotypes of the Old World: a man's rank was clear at a glance. Artisans walked in their leather aprons, farmers in homespun. The people of quality rolled swiftly along in carriages that splashed their inferiors with mud. Tripping delicately into shops, fine ladies had their servants following behind them; merchants were resplendent in imported clothes that aped the Court of Saint James. A few families directed the

[16]

politics of the Colony as members of the King's Council, and kept a stranglehold on its economic life through their control of the meager currency. No wonder some faces were proud, and the manner of an aristocrat with a shopkeeper was brusque.

But a brilliant physiognomist, such as Copley grew to be, would have noticed in the faces of the more well-to-do people, almost hidden under a mask of power and self-confidence, a tinge of worry, as if their position were not quite so secure as they would have liked. Sometimes a King's Counsellor looked quickly away from a man on the street in a shabby greatcoat or a paint-stained apron. For this man had dared to threaten the secret of his power. In 1741, a popular party had swept the provincial elections by advocating that money be based, not on the assets controlled solely by the rich, but on the commodity owned by all, on land. True, the British Parliament had intervened in the nick of time, making the Massachusetts Land Bank illegal and ruining its backers, but the issue would not stay dead. Orators who had called the merchants "merciless usurers," who had accused them of attempting to drive thousands of families into slavery in order to make themselves "lords of manors"; these men were not in jail where, so the aristocrats were convinced, they belonged. These men were still talking. Only a year before, in 1750, after the patrician lieutenant governor, Thomas Hutchinson, had succeeded in passing legislation that barred all paper money, the mob had stormed his house and, when it had caught fire, had cheered, shouting, "Let it burn!"

Such incidents happened only rarely, yet they were symptomatic of a fundamental unrest that was not limited to Boston or the Colonies, but agitated the whole Western world. The old aristocratic system was tottering; it was soon to collapse under the hammer blows of the middle class.

A conflict as basic as this manifests itself in every aspect of life. The same currents that agitated society agitated art. During the centuries of aristocratic dominance, critics had promulgated, on grounds which they insisted were esthetic, the doctrine that an individual's personal peculiarities were less important than the class to which he belonged. To show a ruler as a chinless weakling would be idiotic, since, as a matter of fact, he was the most powerful man in the state. Thus, the portraitists were urged to burn away such trivialities as a man's personal appearance and character, to show rather his social group. The little girl in the fable of the King's Clothes, who startled the bowing courtiers by pointing out that the King was nude, was not only a dangerous revolutionary, but a fool according to the canons of her time. She should have realized that even if a king walked naked, he was beautifully dressed, since elegance of costume was an attribute of kings.

In portraits painted according to the aristocratic philosophy, heads were stylized into masks of rank or beauty, while the emphasis rested on graceful poses, rich settings, sumptuous attire. All the tricks of the painter's art were used to create impressive and harmonious symbols of rank. Had Copley been born in either London or Boston in 1700 rather than 1738, every portraitist of reputation working during his young manhood would have created such pictures as these.

However, the wheel of social evolution, turning ever more rapidly, was bringing to the surface an altogether different social ideal. The middle classes consisted of self-made individuals who lacked rank or social position. They regarded a man's achievements as more important than his birth, his face than his clothes. In London, William Hogarth began during the seventeen-twenties to preach this revolutionary doctrine in paint. His work was so radical that the gentlemen-connoisseurs would not buy his pictures—he made his living from selling prints to the masses; but even fashionable portrait painters like Richardson and Highmore reflected the changing temper of the times by painting a little more realistically than had their predecessor, Sir Godfrey Kneller.

Smibert, the British artist whose trip to America was to mean so much to Copley, occupied a middle ground stylistically. Although he never worked in as downright a manner as Hogarth, the former Edinburgh apprentice failed to achieve that fluent and elegant style that would have made him a successful court painter. Horace Walpole remembered him as "a silent, modest man who abhorred the finesse of his profession." His flight to America was inspired by a combination of disappointment, idealism, and revolt against the empty frivolity of British society painting.

On his arrival in America, Smibert created for his own satisfaction and as a sample of his work a large group portrait of Dean Berkeley's party. Although labored in execution and full of conventional tricks, this picture shows him struggling to catch individuality in faces. Clearly he hoped that the citizens of the New World would permit him to work in a less fashionable style than that demanded by Londoners. At least in part, he was disappointed. The Colonial aristocracy, into which he soon married, was, with all the passion of the new rich, trying to live down its bourgeois origin; leading Bostonians wished to be recorded in the same noble and ideal manner as their betters in England. Smibert's commercial American pictures are an uneasy mixture of frank vision and traditional graces.

Closest of all painters in New England to Smibert was Robert Feke. Styling himself as "mariner" rather than "painter," he was said to have been captured by the Spanish during the War of Jenkins' Ear. His only extant painting from the time before he met Smibert is very unimpressive. But later developments indicate that he had been influenced by the school of painters who, up and down the Hudson River Valley, created handsome and high-spirited portraits based on imported engravings of lords and ladies.

In 1741, he appeared in Smibert's studio. Although never a formal pupil, Feke fell so heavily under Smibert's influence that for a while he made an about-face and struggled to show his Colonial sitters, not as symbols of rank, but as ordinary men. Yet this largely self-taught painter, working in the provincial cities of Boston, Newport, and Philadelphia, was not really satisfied with the middle-class elements he conned from Smibert. Soon he made use of imported engravings to pull himself back into the old channel of court painting.

Feke's mature manner is the most brilliant rendition of the aristocratic ideal produced in Colonial America. His colors are bright, daring, various; his brush strokes free; his long canvases full of sweep and dash. In his compositions, thrusts and counterthrusts add up to harmony. Heads have become elegant abstractions. Bodies also are not particularized; from many a low-cut dress peeps charmingly the same half-hidden left breast. His women are seductive but distant; his men handsome, reserved, austere. Standing in unlocalized landscapes, leaning on classic columns, enjoying the shade of rustic grottoes, these people hardly inhabit the same world as the rest of us. Although Feke disappeared in 1750, when Copley was twelve, the boy was undoubtedly familiar with his work. (Plate 10.)

Feke did not represent the only tendency in American art or American life. The wealthy merchants, who relished the glitter of his mature style, had taken over the control of the Colony early in the century from the Congregational theocracy who had so vigorously opposed worldliness and fine laces. But the ministers and all they stood for were far from being dead. The old Puritan traditions, based on the bourgeois canons of the Old World, now mingled with new revolutionary fire, based on the needs of the rising American middle class. Feke had painted a few divines during his early, sober period, but after he had struck his aristocratic stride the churchmen threw their business to Joseph Badger.

Badger was lowly born, an ingenious artisan. The son of a tailor, he was trained as a house painter and glazier, trades which he never completely abandoned. At about the time of Feke's appearance, he added likenesses to his specialties. Living until 1765, he became, after Feke vanished and Smibert and Pelham died, the leading portraitist of Boston and thus the rival of Copley's early efforts. Like everyone else, Badger accepted the conventional compositions of the period, but when he filtered them through his consciousness, the noble poses adapted from British prints came out as something strange. Although delicately flexed, his ladies' fingers seem less familiar with perfume than dishwater. Each man stands elegantly, but we feel that when the artist finally permits him to relax his pose, he will sigh with relief and unbutton his tight waistcoat. (Plate 10.)

Badger drew badly; his brush was heavy and clumsy some-times. Although his unobtrusive colors were gently harmoni-ous, he was far from being a skillful artist. Yet there is a fascina-tion in his pictures that draws us back to them again and again. Through all the inadequacies of his paint surface there gleam the beginnings of a new vision. The artist depicted men and women, not as symbols, but as real people: just folks. With the hindsight of critics born two centuries later, we can recognize that Badger's approach rather than the approach of Feke rep-resented the directions American history was to follow. But will Copley, the young genius on the verge of launching his ca-reer, see what we see?

Another local artist whose work Copley knew was John Greenwood. He was born to a prosperous and prominent fam-ily, but a reversal in fortunes when he was young resulted in his being apprenticed to Thomas Johnston, an engraver and a painter of fire-buckets who ran up an occasional portrait on the side. Acquiring a little skill in the likeness line, Greenwood abandoned his apprenticeship after a year or two. His son wrote: "He was considered quite a genius for his then quite uncommon productions of the pencil. His company was sought and his time occupied in painting the portraits of his friends."

Greenwood's pictures have all the slapdashness of a self-con-fident youngster, not naturally a painter, who suddenly finds himself admired in an uncritical circle. Stylistically, they fall between Feke and Badger. The elegant compositions of the former become quick, geometric patterns. In losing their sen-suousness, they tip over to the intellectual side of the scale and thus approach Badger's homely vernacular. There is little thought or care in the work of this artist who was soon to give up painting altogether and become an art dealer in London. Copley had least to learn from Greenwood, yet that prodigy was a family friend. (Plate 10.)

Had Copley, as he prepared to practice his craft, been enabled by some magic to read what I have just written, he would have been puzzled and quite possibly enraged at the way I have linked social and esthetic considerations. "Political contests," he was to insist, are "neither pleasing to an artist or advantageous to the art itself." All through his career he tried to hold himself aloof from the currents of controversy that moved his world. Yet, despite his best efforts, he became actively involved in the beginnings of the Revolution. Although unconsciously, his art was also embroiled.

The teen-age boy undoubtedly phrased his problem in very personal terms. His family required his financial help; his training pointed toward engraving and painting; he must start as quickly as possible to turn out a salable product. Abstract esthetic considerations, so later letters reveal, bothered him as little as philosophic ones. He went at learning his trade much as a saddler or coachmaker would. You began, of course, by studying such models as you could find. Available to Copley were the works of his predecessors in Boston, a few imported portraits, some inferior copies of European masterpieces, and a considerable number of engravings after both the likenesses and the subject pictures of the Old World. From a combination of these raw materials he attempted to build pictures of his own.

Greenwood's career has shown us that it was possible to achieve success as a portraitist in Boston by turning out zestfully a slapdash product, but Copley's temperament was the opposite

of Greenwood's. He bent over his canvases in an agony of in-
decision. Every feature he painted was questioned, rubbed out
a dozen times, and then allowed to remain only because the
picture had to be finished. If the boy whose childhood had
been a round of terror possessed any self-confidence, it was the
grim determination of the frightened who fight lest they perish.

It was natural that his earliest known canvases, painted when
he was about fifteen, show little personality and are, indeed,
mutually contradictory. Very ambitious was his group portrait
of four Gore children. (Plate 12.) That the picture gives a finished impression is probably due to the fact that the artist
copied some engraving by rote. The young sitters have identical pretty faces, which show no observation of nature, and the
landscape in the background is a confectioner's concoction,
complete with ornamental bridge and sailboat. Each child's
dress is painted a different bright color: one yellow, one blue,
one pink, one tobacco-brown. The picture shows that Copley
had great natural skill as a painter, but that for the moment he
was applying it to nothing of his own.

Painting and engraving a portrait of a well-known Congregational minister, the Reverend William Welsteed, presented a
different problem. Remembering that Badger was the painter
par excellence of ministers, Copley turned out a most Badger-
esque likeness, a grave, unadorned picture. A commission to
make companion canvases of a fashionable young couple, Mr.
and Mrs. Joseph Mann, called for a third solution.   (Plate 13.)
He borrowed, probably from English engravings, compositions
of conventional elegance. The execution seems an amalgam of
Smibert and Feke, with perhaps a touch of Greenwood. Bright
colors are piled on next to one another in a most amateurish

manner. Like all of Copley's early works, the pictures give a spurious impression of finish, yet an occasional detail stands out as crude because the artist has suddenly been caught by an observation of nature and tried to draw something for himself.

Copley was floundering, like an inexperienced navigator who changes his course for every puff of breeze, when suddenly a great wind arose. In 1754 or 1755, there appeared in Boston an itinerant portrait painter, Joseph Blackburn, who practiced a somewhat primitive variation of the most fancy of all contemporary English portrait styles. Almost a signature is the way he covers his ladies, as if they were Christmas trees, with looping festoons of pearls. He had a gift for graceful poses, quite unlike the stiff mannerisms of the local artists, and he showed an almost feminine affection for laces and satins. His palette was sensitive, glowing, instinct with charm. But his portraits lack strength: men and women alike are given faces that are weak and characterless. Unlike the sober and heavy Smibert, Blackburn, the lyricist, reflected wholeheartedly the aristocratic thinking of the past.

Although Copley, who was doing portraits on his own, could never have been Blackburn's apprentice, he enthusiastically imitated the newcomer's virtues, not hesitating to borrow entire conceptions if they pleased him. When Blackburn painted Mary Sylvester Dering as a shepherdess, with a crook in her hand and a lamb by her side, Copley did the same for one of his sitters, Ann Tyng. (Plate 11.) By such means he quickly assimilated much of the grace of his elder's style, and then he was the better painter, for, as continuing success gave him more self-confidence, he developed increasingly in directions of his own.

He could not refuse to borrow Blackburn's jewels and gestures and elaborate backgrounds—were they not the latest rage from London?—but then he could not fail to use his own eyes as well. Although he did not consciously recognize the fact, the Colonial master reflected the preconceptions of the revolutionary class into which he was born. He was fundamentally a realist. Fine clothes were nice things to have and very suitable things to paint, but he himself was much more interested in character in faces. While still under Blackburn's shadow, he painted *General William Brattle* (Plate 15), a real man standing heavily in an ordinary world. The gold braid on his buff waistcoat, the ceremonial sword, the daintily pointing fingers of his right hand; all these fail to draw our eyes away from the grave and powerful face.

By the time he was nineteen, Copley's fame had traveled so far that he was invited to Nova Scotia. "There are several people who would be glad to employ you," wrote Thomas Ainslie of Halifax. "I believe so because I have heard it mentioned." Copley, however, did not go; perhaps the idea of travel terrified him.

The boy who had huddled behind locked doors on Long Wharf had become a self-contained young man who worked at his trade with passionate intensity and rarely went out in the world. The popular historical novelist who depicted him as turning up at a drunken brawl at Harvard and taking the blame when the college authorities intervened could hardly have distorted his character further from what the evidence shows. By nature afraid of his fellow men, painfully conscious that he practiced a socially inferior profession, Copley carried sober respectability to the extreme. The worst aberration that is recorded against him is that a selectman once caught him strolling on the

Sabbath. Gravely he explained that he worked so hard during the week he had to take exercise on Sunday for his health.

Copley's labors were not made easier by any self-complacency. He was conscious that his hand could record only a little of what his eyes saw. Toiling by the hour to invent answers to problems which he was sure the old masters had solved, he cursed the misfortune that had given him no good models to study. He was to tell his children that he had been entirely self-taught and had never seen a first-rate picture while a young man. He was to write Benjamin West: "In this country, as you rightly observe, there is no example of art except what is to [be] met with in a few prints indifferently executed, from which it is not possible to learn much. . . . I think myself particularly unlucky in living in a place into which there has not been one portrait brought that is worthy to be called a picture within my memory, which leaves me at a great loss to guess the style that you, Mr. Reynolds, and other artists practice."

Pieces of information that he gleaned from books stuck in his mind like burrs, demanding action. He read that people drew pictures in pastel, a kind of crayon. This seemed a good idea, but there were no suitable crayons in America. After, we may be sure, a long inward battle with his shyness, he wrote to the man the books said was the greatest living pastelist. He asked the Swiss, Jean-Etienne Liotard, who was famous for such sentimental pieces as his *Chocolate Girl,* now in the Dresden Gallery, to send him "one set of crayons of the very best kind, such as you can recommend [for] liveliness, color, and justness of tints. . . . You may perhaps be surprised that so remote a corner of the globe as New England should have any demand for the necessary utensils for practicing the fine arts, but I assure you, sir, however feeble our efforts may be, it is not for want of inclination that they are not better, but the want of opportunity to improve ourselves. However, America, which has been the seat of war and desolation, I would fain hope will one day become the school of fine arts, and Monsieur Liotard['s] drawings with justice be set as patterns for our imitation." It was a nice compliment, but Copley was too truthful to keep from adding: "Not that I have ever had the advantage of beholding any one of these rare pieces from your hand, but [have] formed a judgment on the true taste of several of my friend who has seen [th]em." There is no indication that Liotard ever answered Copley's letter, but the young man secured crayons somewhere and became America's earliest important draftsman in pastel.

Working in crayons gave Copley a refreshing feeling of release, for, as he employed this lighter and quicker medium, he was able to forget temporarily the profound problems that made his oil paintings an agonizing battle to record the basic forms of nature, the basic traits of humanity. His pastels are decorative, brightly colored, and for him superficial. He depicted Thomas Hancock both in crayon and oil. When making the drawing, Copley shaped the features smoothly and broadly, creating a likeness that would be recognized by a friend, but would give a stranger little idea of character. The painted head (Plate 23) contains many more details, many more shapes and planes, yet is more completely realized in the round. We see before us a vainglorious, shrewd, and stubborn fat man, the very merchant who ran up a few pounds into a great fortune.

Copley's pastel self-portrait (Plate 9), showing him at about the age of twenty-two, is on the whole disappointing. The smooth, heavy face reflects but dimly the intense, humorless,

passionate, and restrained personality of the artist. Copley pre-
fered to concentrate on depicting the fine silk of his lounging
robe and the elaborate stuff of his waistcoat. Yet the uncom-
municativeness of this portrait can only be blamed in part on
the pastel medium. Copley never dissected himself as he dissected others; the oil self-portrait he painted many years later
in England is more revealing than the crayon drawing, it is
true, but not a really profound likeness. How unintrospective
Copley was is shown by his belief, expressed in a letter to West,
that his pastels were among his best pictures, a belief inspired,
we may assume, less by the drawings themselves than by the
carefree pleasure he had in creating them.

As in the case of his early self-portrait, Copley often copied
heads from his bigger likenesses in watercolor on tiny chips of
ivory; he also made miniatures for which he had no large
models. (Plate 14.) Such pictures as his *Nathaniel Hurd* here
illustrated are done in oil on small plates of copper. Meant to
be personal keepsakes more intimate than full-size portraits,
the little likenesses needed no more than suggest the presence
of a loved one. Copley tended to indicate the general shape of
a head, add the most obvious features, and then consider the
portrait complete. The figures crowd the frames in the typical
eighteenth century manner, and the shoulders drop in steep
lines that have little relation to nature but make a satisfactory
design. Copley, who was a rugged artist, seems not to have been
really interested in delicacy and a small scale, yet he was too
able to do anything badly. His little oils on copper are sometimes surprisingly strong, and his true miniatures, with their
harmonious details and their fresh color, rank with the best
created by his Colonial contemporaries.

[30]

Before many years had passed, Copley abandoned miniature painting altogether, as bringing too low a price, for his increasing fame had brought him sitters of higher social position until his studio was filled with the most prosperous citizens of Boston. The depression that had followed the French and Indian War was over, and the bright sun of prosperity seemed to have shriveled up the Popular Party of men like Samuel Adams, who a few years before had almost started an insurrection in the name of a land bank and cheap money. The many-headed were silent; not the smallest cloud in the sky indicated that the country would soon be torn by revolution. In refusing another invitation to Halifax, Copley wrote during 1765: "I have a large room full of pictures unfinished which would engage me these twelve months if I did not begin any others. . . . I assure you I have been as fully employed these several years past as I could expect or wish to be, as more would be a means to retard the design I have always had in view, that of improving in that charming art which is my delight, and gaining a reputation, rather than a fortune without that."

Copley, however, was not indifferent to the sums he earned, for he had known poverty too well in his youth not to recognize its power of bringing unhappiness, and he knew that in the materialistic Colonies he could command respect only if he became rich. The low opinion in which Americans held art filled him with anger. "Was it not," he wrote, "for preserving the resemblance of particular persons, painting would not be known in the place. The people generally regard it no more than any other useful trade, as they sometimes term it, like that of a carpenter, tailor, or shrew-maker [shoe-maker?], not as one of the most noble arts in the world. Which is not a little mortifying to me. While the arts are so disregarded, I can hope for nothing either to encourage or assist me in my studies but what I receive from a thousand leagues' distance, and be my improvements what they will, I shall not be benefited by them in this country, neither in point of fortune nor fame."

In his yearning for contact with European taste, Copley studied engravings after fashionable English portraits. Actually, these imported models menaced his art. There in his Boston painting room, he went through a personal temptation of Saint Anthony. His genius, the instincts that had been molded in Colonial Boston, were good angels urging him not to raise his eyes from the book of reality. But around him, so seductive, so full of glitter and charm, floated the aristocratic visions of the Old World. "Paint like me," whispered the engraving after Hudson in tones of honey. "Imitate this ruffle, this grandly looped curtain, and I will give you a whole world of taste and fame." And when Copley's sitters entered his studio, only too often they joined forces with temptation in their longing to be made to look like lords and ladies.

Not a saint nor yet a devil, Copley did not resolve the problem violently one way or the other. He did not rise in mighty wrath to throw the harlots from him, nor did he follow them away from the solid world in which his spirit lived. He mixed together the old and the new, the foreign and the homespun; and amazingly these seeming irreconcilables lay down peacefully side by side. For the fancy and the plain were mingled in his own temperament and in the temperaments of his sitters even as they were mingled in his art.

That strong painting hand performed strange marriages. In his Colonial embarrassment, Copley hated to paint the women of Boston in the clothes they really wore. He was to complain to West that in order to dress his women in the latest styles, he would have to import the gowns himself from England. He copied exactly a print after Reynolds, even to the hairy little dog in the sitter's arms and the number of pearls in her hair; then he interpolated the face of a Boston matron, Mrs. Jerathmael Bowers. He created three portraits—*Mrs. John Amory, Mrs. John Murray,* and *Mrs. Daniel Hubbard*—whose almost identical compositions are almost identical with that of *Henrietta, Countess of Suffolk,* by an unidentified minor English artist; probably all four had a common engraved source. Copley's likeness of Elizabeth Ross (c. 1767) follows closely one of the two figures in Reynolds' *Ladies Amabel and Mary Jemima Yorke,* of which several engravings had been made. (Plate 11.) The picture was not one of Copley's best, but it is a remarkable tribute to the verisimilitude of his brush that even such canvases carry with them some accent of truth. And when in the heat of creation he forgot he was painting crude persons in a crude technique, his portraits reveal great strength and sincerity of personal vision, as his likeness of Epes Sargent shows.

Sargent was a merchant of great wealth. He owned ten of the transatlantic and fishing ships whose sails enlivened the blue of Boston Harbor, and he looked on Sam Adams's rabble with such disdain that when the Revolution got under way, he was one of the royalists singled out for special persecution. Trying to paint this great man in a manner suited to his position, Copley imagined a truncated column and told Sargent to lean on one elbow in a graceful pose. The conception of the picture was thus suitably elegant, but the execution went completely wrong according to aristocratic standards. Instead of leaning like a willow bent by a perfumed breeze, the merchant is shown as a heavy man, whose weight, bearing down on his elbow, will soon force him to change his position. In the hand Sargent holds before his breast, the fingers are suitably spread for a decorative effect, but Copley became so fascinated with the thick fleshiness of the powerful fingers that he painted them exactly as they were. They are almost obscenely full of blood and life. The face, too, is more instinct with truth than beauty. (Plates 18 and 19.)

From imported engravings, Copley could imitate poses, costumes, and compositions, but he was forced to work out for himself, by the laborious process of trial and error, those aspects of technique most valuable in achieving shape and verisimilitude and a painterly effect. The expedients he achieved were driven deep into his consciousness by successive acts of creation. His figures, though clumsy and occasionally faulty in drawing, had a solidity not to be found in the work of many of his more brilliant English contemporaries; they looked as if they had been hewn with an axe from the hard wood of American forests. What if the silk of his sitters' gowns lacked the soft sheen of silk, but seemed rather a hard, solid substance carved by the woodcutter into folds that would remain immovable for centuries? This, too, added to the strength and inevitability of the impression.

Able to secure few hints on coloring from abroad, for color printing had not been invented and the copies of European pictures he saw were usually very inaccurate, Copley was forced to work out his own palette. Many of his paintings are experiments in tones; some miserable failures, some brilliant successes whose originality and skill take one's breath away. Finally he developed a personal palette: cool metallic colors; greens and tans and russets and grays laid on smoothly over large surfaces. There is none of the tinkling of little lights, none of the brilliant contrasts, none of the bravura work of the British school. His color, evolved by the same anguish from the same mind as his brushwork, his drawing, and his characterization, blended with them to give an impression of great power.

Before he was twenty-five, Copley had achieved a mature style. His manner was solid, not flashy; it was slow and profound. According to European standards it was naïve, clumsy even, yet it was strong and straight as those wilderness trees which the king's agents marked for use as the masts of frigates.

There on canvas are the diverse citizens of the New World, man and woman not corseted to any pattern, but allowed to expand to their true stature. Mr. and Mrs. Benjamin Pickman were a young couple of wealth and fashion, the kind of patricians who should, according to the imported conventions that Copley knew, have been shown standing, aloof and noble and cold, before a tasteful background removed by the generalizing alchemy of the painter's brush from the ordinary world. Mrs. Pickman, it is true, is given a backdrop of masonry to stand before, but she does not belong there any more than we plebeian onlookers do. A very real sun is plotting to freckle her nose, and she is lifting against it, in the most natural of gestures, a blue-green umbrella. The nose itself shows a pug that takes it far from a drawing master's ideal of noses, while the total face is that of a not too attractive matron who will, unless she is careful of her diet, soon be much too fat. Her expression, far from showing nobility and disdain, is that of a comfortable housewife who enjoys a good gossip, even with her own maid. Her pose is so matter-of-fact that it takes no imagination to visualize her stepping out into the room beside us.   (Plate 2.)

Her husband is a lanky, spider-like man. The sweet disorder in his dress is perhaps intended to be nonchalant, but it comes through rather as easy informality. Here, admittedly, is a handsome face, but we do not have to look hard to see under the correct features the shrewdness which enabled this Tory, although driven into exile, to come out of the Revolution richer than he went in.   (Plate 3.)

Turning to the other political camp, we observe Copley's likeness of the archradical, James Otis. (Plate 5.) The picture is painted with choppy, almost brutal, brushstrokes that leave ridges of paint—a style which the artist employed for a short time about 1760. Otis sits heavily, with his knees outspread. His face, done in bright flesh tones and bluish shadows, wears a mask of gravity and calm, but the hand that holds a book is clasped with nervous tension, and the whole body seems to stay in its chair only with considerable strain. Otis is about to leap up in an impassioned outburst. We are not surprised to read in our history books that this man's nerves eventually got the better of his sanity.

Copley's painting manner had become finished in its very crudeness. His range, it is true, was narrow technically, but the effects he attempted he achieved with great skill. Perhaps because his instruction had come so largely from engravings, he was inclined to think in terms of black and white. In his portrait of Mrs. Nathaniel Appleton (Plate 18), he not only accepted this limitation but gloried in it. A sharp eye will notice that Mrs. Appleton's sleeve is not black but dark green; that the chair and the table cover are not gray but a muffled red. Yet these low tints are incidental to the non-chromatic pattern set up by the contrast between the white costume and the black shawl. Light and shadow, carefully studied from a single source of radiance and not greatly modified by middle tones, heighten the black-and-white effect and give a strong impression of plasticity. The shapes are strong, full, and inevitable. It would be hard to imagine a picture that had a greater impact of reality.

At twenty-five, an age when most painters now alive are hardly out of art school, the self-taught Copley had already become the greatest painter ever to work in Colonial America, and one of the most interesting artists of his world generation.

THREE

Advice by Letter

COPLEY, who had trusted his own intellect only because he could find no models to copy, was not conscious of his skill; always he felt that, if he could see the work of the old masters he had read about, his own pictures would be proved worthless. Even moderns like West and Reynolds, he believed, must paint twice as well as he. When he heard that some of West's pictures had been imported to Philadelphia, he considered journeying to see them, but despite his passionate desire for self-improvement, he did not go. Was this due to the fear of traveling that haunted him all his life, or to the fear that he would find his own art vastly inferior?

Copley's timidity hampered him in all his contacts with the world; he was so afraid of his fellow men that he never had a friend. His intimates were always in his family circle, which was now made up of his ailing mother and his much younger half-brother, Henry Pelham. For the rest, there was the long succession of sitters who streamed into his studio, but with them he had only formal intercourse. The seeker for perfection

[37]

struggled so hard with his medium that he never talked while
he painted, and had he talked, who would have understood
him? His mind was engrossed in an art most Bostonians considered a menial trade. No one in the whole city, Copley felt,
was capable of appreciating what he was trying to do, and he
was overcome by a sense of loneliness when his good pictures
were not distinguished from his bad, when the Colonials com-
mented only on the likeness, that being, as Copley complained,
"the main part of the excellence of a portrait in the opinion of
our New England connoisseurs."

Perhaps he could have escaped his isolation by surrounding
himself with young men who wanted to paint, eager young
craftsmen whom he could have fired with his own aspirations
and ideals. A few such called on him, but were not encouraged;
in his entire life he never had a pupil except his half-brother.
He may have dreamed of a woman who would love and understand him, but he certainly was very shy with the ladies. When
one of his kinsmen married, the contrast with his own loneliness
depressed him deeply; only a desire to reach perfection in his
art, he wrote, has "given me the resolution to live a bachelor to
the age of twenty-eight. However, I don't despair but I shall
be married, as I find miracles don't cease."

Certainly his loneliness, his desire for intelligent intercourse,
helped to overcome his fears so far that in 1766 he sent a portrait
of his half-brother to London for submission to the Society
of Artists. (Plate 1.) However, as soon as he had entrusted
his *Boy with Squirrel* to Captain Bruce, he regretted having
done so. He wrote that he half-hoped the sea voyage had so
changed the colors that the picture could not be exhibited, and
"I may not have the mortification of hearing of its being con-

demned. I confess I am under some apprehension of its not being so much esteemed as I could wish. I don't say this to induce you to be backward in letting me know how far it is judged to deserve censure, for I can truly say, if I know my own heart, I am less anxious to enjoy than deserve applause."

Captain Bruce was slow in notifying Copley how the picture was received, but the painter heard from other sources that "none but the works of the first masters were ranked with it. . . . This is an encouragement to me, I confess, and adds new vigor to the pencil." Jubilantly, he wrote West to say that he was delighted to have the approval of one "from whom America receives the same luster that Italy does from her Titiano and divine Raphael." Of course he had never seen a picture by any of the three artists he compared, but how, in his excitement, could he resist citing the great names he had seen in books? He begged West to correspond with him.

Finally a boat brought Copley two letters. The one from Captain Bruce, having repeated Reynolds's praises, added that the English master had criticized the hardness and overminuteness of the drawing, the coldness of the colors. The other letter was from West himself; it too was full of encouragement, though West wrote that the connoisseurs generally had thought the picture too "liny . . . which indeed, as far as I was capable of judging, was somewhat the case, for I very well know that from endeavoring at great correctness in one's outline, it is apt to produce a poverty in the look of one's works. . . . For in nature everything is round . . . which makes it impossible that nature, when seen in light and shade, can ever appear liny." Both West and Reynolds urged Copley to come to Europe before his style had hardened into its provincial mold.

"You have got to that length in the art," West wrote, "that nothing is wanted to perfect you now but a sight of what has been done by the great masters, and if you would make a visit to Europe for this purpose for three or four years, you would find yourself then in possession of what will be highly valuable. . . . You may depend on my friendship in any way that's in my power to serve."

West was able to advise Copley out of his own experience. The two men had been born in the same year on the provincial shores of America. The son of a rural Pennsylvania innkeeper, West had also begun to draw as a small child. This strange activity attracted attention. A guest at his father's inn gave him paints; soon he was called to the neighboring metropolis of Lancaster, and then to Philadelphia, where he created portraits that were greatly admired. Up to this point his style, like Copley's, had developed in semi-isolation, but now the gentlemen of the most cultured of American cities intervened. The Philadelphians took up a subscription to send their local genius abroad. Reaching Italy at the age of twenty-two, West absorbed the teachings of the Old World so successfully that the art critics of Rome dubbed him "the American Raphael." When he carried to London an amalgam of European and American styles, Fame rode with him in the coach. By the time Copley sent over his *Boy with Squirrel,* West had achieved worldly power through his close friendship with George III, and was regarded by the connoisseurs in many lands as the painter most likely to restore to the art the glory and dignity of the old masters.

At last in communication with someone he felt would understand, Copley poured out in letters to West complaints about lack of taste in America and the scarcity of good pictures to study. Then he begged his new friend to explain various points that had puzzled him in books on painting. "I shall be exceeding glad," he wrote, "to know in general what the present state of painting in Italy is; whether the living masters are excellent as the dead have been. It is not possible my curiosity can be satisfied in this by anybody but yourself, not having any correspondence with any whose judgment is sufficient to satisfy me."

Taking to heart all the criticisms West and Reynolds had sent him, Copley determined to obviate them all in the full length of a little girl that he painted for the next London exhibition. Since Reynolds had called his colors cold, he used bright tints he did not feel, and in an attempt to keep the figure from standing out in a manner that could be called "liny," he made the background very conspicuous, confusing the picture with a red-figured Turkey rug, a scarlet curtain, a yellow chair, a spaniel, and a green-and-yellow parrot. Although his portrait of Mary Warner (Plate 19) was one of the least sincere he had ever done, he sent it off with a sense of self-satisfaction.

West wrote him that on the whole it had been less well received than the *Boy with Squirrel*. "Your picture is in possession of drawing to a correctness that is very surprising, and of coloring very brilliant, though this brilliancy is somewhat misapplied, as for instance the gown too bright for the flesh." Each part of the canvas, he added, was of equal strength in tint and finish, without due subordination to the principal parts. "These are criticisms I should not make was not your pictures very nigh upon a footing with the first artists who now paints." Again he urged Copley to come to Europe, promising to put him up in his own London house and to give him introductions to all the principal Italian connoisseurs. Letters from Captain

Bruce notified him of his election to the Society of Artists, and also importuned him to come abroad before it was too late.

The advisability of crossing the ocean now stared Copley in the face. He had long mourned the lack of opportunities for self-improvement in America, and now, since his new picture had been considered inferior to the *Boy with Squirrel*, he was forced to recognize that he could not profit from criticism by letter. In addition, he was most favorably situated for a European trip: he was a member of the London Society of Artists; West, the King's painter, invited him to stay; he would meet all the most famous Italian connoisseurs.

Yet Copley did not jump at the chance; in his imagination, the roads of Europe swarmed with bandits eager to cut his throat. Many years later, he was to write from abroad: "It [is] curious to observe that in all the places that I have [been] in, men seem to be the same set of being, rather disposed to oblige and be civil than otherwise. . . . Robberies are very rarely known to be perpetrated. . . . I do not find those dangers and difficulties . . . so great as people do that sit at home and paint out frightful stories to themselves in their imaginations. . . . I find all the difficulty is in setting about such business." But in the seventeen-sixties he had not yet learned this lesson.

Financial terror joined with physical fear to make Copley put behind him his desire to excel in his art for the joy of excelling. Supposing he did study in Europe, he asked in an incompleted draft of a letter probably intended for Captain Bruce, "what shall I do at the end of that time (for prudence bids us to consider the future as well as the present)? Why, I must either return to America and bury all my improvements among people entirely destitute of all just ideas of the arts, and without any addition of reputation to what I have already gained . . . or I should set down in London in a way perhaps less advantageous than what I am in at present, and I cannot think of purchasing fame at so dear a rate."

In another letter to Bruce, Copley harps on the same theme: "I would gladly exchange my situation for the serene climate of Italy, or even that of England, but what would be the advantage of seeking improvement at such an outlay of time and money? I am now in as good business as the poverty of this place will admit. I make as much money as if I were a Raphael or a Correggio, and three hundred guineas a year, my present income, is equal to nine hundred a year in London. With regard to reputation, you are sensible that fame cannot be durable where pictures are confined to sitting rooms, and regarded only for the resemblance they bear to their originals. Were I sure of doing as well in Europe as here, I would not hesitate a moment in my choice, but I might in the experiment waste a thousand pounds and two years of my time, and have to return baffled to America. Then I should have to take my mother with me, who is ailing. She does not, however, seem averse to cross the salt water once more, but my failure would oblige her to recross the sea again. My ambition whispers me to run this risk, and I think the time draws nigh that must determine my future fortune."

Copley wrote West that he was sending him two pictures that would show improvements he had recently made. The subject of one would be in England; he asked West to compare the sitter to his likeness and decide whether Copley could expect to make his living as a portrait painter in London. "I must beg, however, that you will not suffer your benevolent wishes for my welfare to induce you to think more favorably of my works than they deserve." He had concluded that it would not be worth his while to go abroad unless he would not have to return to America.

When West's reply came, it showed the court painter was puzzled by Copley's materialistic attitude. The old masters, he wrote, "to a man of powers . . . are a source of knowledge ever to be prized and sought after. I would, therefore, Mr. Copley, advise your making this visit while young and before you determine to settle. I don't apprehend it needs be more than one year, as you won't go in pursuit of that which you are not advanced in, but as a satisfaction to yourself hereafter in knowing to what length the art has been carried. By this you will find yourself in possession of powers you will then feel, that cannot be communicated by words." West added that in the candid opinion of the connoisseurs "you have nothing to hazard in coming to this place," but advised Copley not to make up his mind whether he would stay in England until he had finished his studies.

Copley did not answer this letter or send any more pictures to be exhibited in London. A new interest had joined with the discouragement of West's equivocal message to turn his eyes back to his Colonial homeland. The new interest was love.

FOUR

Golden Years

WHEN A POOR BOY on Long Wharf, Copley had watched the
great merchants strut to their warehouses, dressed in imported
clothes, radiating the self-confidence of those who are born to
command. And when one of them deigned to walk into Mrs.
Copley's tobacco shop, how his mother curtsied behind the
counter, how the lad stared with grave-eyed wonder at such
magnificence! The painter had been born into the class from
which Sam Adams's revolutionary rabble was recruited. During his early professional years, he seems to have sided with the
radical party. References in his letters to the Stamp-Act riots
reveal that his sympathy had been with the mob which sacked
the houses of the rich.

As time passed, however, the humbly born limner was increasingly taken up by the social and political rulers of Boston.
In his eagerness for self-improvement, he had modeled his
manners on those of his more elegant sitters, till no one could
tell he had not been born into the Colonial aristocracy. When
he had been younger, we gather from his early self-portraits, his

[45]

square face had been too fat, the hair growing down too low over his forehead, but now, although he had not thinned down into the handsome man he was to become in middle age, the shapelessness of his face was giving way to a look of stubborn power, a bulldog look which successful merchants must have found more impressive than graceful beauty. Although his brown-gray eyes gleamed with intelligence, they did not flit from object to object with mercurial rapidity; they fixed in a long, intense stare. Probably he spoke slowly and with deliberation, the words heavy with thought. (Plates 9 and 14.)

It was plain that Copley was sober and hard-working, and the number of his commissions indicated that he was making a good income. When he called at fine houses to arrange for portraits, his sitters got in the habit of asking him to stop in the drawing room, and soon it seemed natural for him to call when he had no portrait to paint. Sitting with his legs comfortably stretched under an imported table, a cup of the best China tea in his hand, he found himself chatting as an equal with gentlemen who had stared through him when he was his mother's errand boy. In such surroundings, he forgot his ambition to study in Europe; Benjamin West's advice faded from his mind while he heard wealthy men talk of cargo and the King's Council.

Naturally Copley was impressed by the delicate and accomplished women he now met, so different from the hoydens of the waterfront. One in particular appealed to him. Susannah Clarke, the daughter of a rich Tory merchant, had a gentle smile that made him feel at home in the luxury of her drawing room. She was handsome, but not with the cold, flashing beauty of the great belles; under soft blue-gray eyes her chin receded gently toward a soft white neck. However, she was nobody's fool and this impressed the painter too; her overlarge nose jutted out strong with deeply etched nostrils; her brow was high under the upsweep of her fashionably piled hair; and the words she spoke in a harmonious voice were clever. Copley must have known it was foolhardy for the son of a tobacconist to fall in love with the daughter of Richard Clarke, but surely his eyes did not deceive him, surely her lips smiled when he came into the room, surely she listened with interest to his passionate talk of art, to his hungry aspirations. When at last he found the courage to propose, she accepted. Probably her father was not enthusiastic about the match, but Copley was able to show that he was a hard workman in a profitable line of business which netted him three hundred guineas a year. On November 16, 1769, he married into one of the leading Tory families of Boston.

Faced with the responsibility of providing an elegant home for his elegant bride, Copley put behind him all thought of going to Europe. Perhaps he was ashamed of this, for when he wanted information about a special kind of oil paint, he wrote, not to West, but to an indifferent practitioner who had emigrated from Boston to the Barbados.

His rich marriage helped his business. Soon he had invested some three thousand dollars in a twenty-acre farm with three houses on it, which took in most of what is now Beacon Hill, but was then, according to a contemporary account, "exactly like country, with trees, bushes, shrubs, and flowers." It was a magnificent site, suitable to a prosperous gentleman. His next-door neighbor was John Hancock, one of the richest men in Boston, whose mansion was a show place of the city. Copley's front windows looked out on the Common, and his back windows over the water to the hills of Brookline beyond. Many hundreds of acres that are now Back Bay had not been filled in; where the best families now live, their ancestral codfish swam.

A year after his marriage, Copley had a daughter; he seemed tied to Boston and Colonial respectability forever, but under his feet a rumble of earthquake grew daily louder. In order to stop mob intimidation of the Royal Commissioners of Customs, the British Government had sent two regiments of regulars to Boston, where their presence stirred mounting bad feeling. Sam Adams published atrocity stories accusing them of beating babies and raping young girls; anyone might share the grief of the venerable patriarch who "the other morning discovered a soldier in bed with his favorite granddaughter." The patriots haled the soldiers into court on every pretext, while the soldiers hustled their tormentors around, pricking them with bayonets. On March 5, 1770, some small boys snowballed a sentry on King Street. When he frightened them away with his bayonet, an angry mob gathered; the sentry called the main guard. Its arrival drew hoots from the crowd, and then a shower of missiles. Losing their heads, the troops fired, killing five civilians. The famous Boston Massacre had taken place.

Conscious that an engraving of the massacre would have a large sale, Copley's pupil and half-brother, Henry Pelham, designed one immediately and sent a proof to Paul Revere, the silversmith who made the frames for Copley's pictures. When Revere published his own print of the tragedy, the one that is reproduced in millions of schoolbooks and is probably the best-known print ever made in America, Pelham wrote him the following letter:

Sir,

When I heard that you was cutting a plate of the late murder, I thought it impossible, as I knew you was not capable of doing it unless you copied it from mine, and as I thought I had entrusted it in the hands of a person who had more regard to the dictates of honor and justice than to take the undue advantage you have done of the confidence and trust I reposed in you. But I find I was mistaken, and after being at the great trouble and expense of making a design, paying for paper, printing, etc., I find myself in the most ungenerous manner deprived not only of any proposed advantage, but even of the expense I have been at, as truly as if you had plundered me on the highway. If you are insensible at the dishonor you have brought on yourself by this act, the world will not be so. However, I leave you to reflect upon and consider one of the most dishonorable actions you could well be guilty of.

H. PELHAM

P.S. I send by the bearer the prints I borrowed of you. My mother desired you would send the hinges and part of the press that you had from her.

Revere's engraving of the Boston Massacre overshadowed Pelham's, of which only two examples have come down to the present.

The shooting of unarmed citizens had so enraged the Boston patriots that militia companies sprang up by spontaneous generation, and a citizens' army was soon drilling on the Common under Copley's windows. Every evening, just as twilight put a stop to the painter's labors, the air was riven with the shrill whistle of fifes and the menacing pound of drums. Round and round, back and forth, the apprentices and dock hands maneuvered clumsily, fowling pieces on their shoulders. The tramp of many feet shook the floor of Copley's living room, and the peaceable artist's heart shrank within him. "I avoid engaging in politics," he wrote to his wife some years later, "as I wish to preserve an undisturbed mind and a tranquillity inconsistent with political disputes." He was not stirred by martial tunes; he hated the idea of slaughter. Looking from the window of his fine mansion at the young men drilling below, he felt again the fear and horror he had known as a small boy when he peered from the window of his mother's shop at the rowdies gouging out each other's eyes on Long Wharf.

It was during these troubled times that he received a letter from John Greenwood, his former rival, who had given up painting and become a successful picture dealer in London. Greenwood said that city was the artistic center of the world, and that "West goes on painting like a Raphael"; he then commissioned Copley to do a portrait of his aged mother and send it across the ocean to him. He suggested that Copley allow him to show it at the newly founded Royal Academy, which now overshadowed the Society of Artists where Copley had previously exhibited.

Thus prodded, Copley's thoughts returned to Europe. After he had completed the picture, he wrote again to West: "I am afraid you will think I have been negligent in suffering two years to pass without exhibiting something, or writing to you to let you know how the art goes on this side of the Atlantic." Having, as usual, complained of the lack of opportunity in America "to prosecute any work of fancy for want of materials," he blamed his marriage and his sick mother for keeping him in so unpropitious a place. "Yet be assured, notwithstanding I have entered into engagements that have retarded my traveling, they shall not finally prevent it."

Copley was always overcome with terror when in his mind's eye he tried to compare his portraits with the fabled portraits of the Old World. He confided to West that Greenwood's intention of exhibiting the portrait of his mother at the Royal Academy filled him with apprehension. The lady was so old that her likeness might make a bad impression; he would like to show as contrast "a subject in the bloom of youth." However, he could not do so unless he used a picture already in England in the possession of John Wilkes, the famous radical. Would people, he asked, assume therefore that he agreed with Wilkes's politics? "I would not have it at the exhibition on any account whatever if there is the least reason to suppose it would give offense to any person of either party." West did not show the picture.

While waiting for his friend's reply, Copley made his first long journey; he rode to New York. "The city," he wrote in the words of a true New Englander, "has more grand buildings than Boston, the streets much cleaner and some much broader, but it is not Boston in my opinion yet." He stayed six months, painting about seven hundred pounds' worth of portraits. The most substantial people flocked to his studio, and even those who had been abroad, he boasted, said his were the best pictures they had ever seen. Copley rose at six, breakfasted at eight, painted until three, when he dined, and at six rode out. "I hardly get time to eat my victuals. . . . It takes up much time to finish all the parts of a picture when it is to be well finished, and the gentry of this place distinguish very well, so I must slight nothing." He missed the assistance of Henry Pelham, who usually helped him by laying in backgrounds.

But Copley was making money and that kept him cheerful; he realized the value of money as only a man who has known poverty can. "You can depend on it," he wrote to his half-brother, "I shall not send my letter in a cover, because the postage will be double if I should." Concerning a lawsuit which Pelham was handling for him, he warned: "Don't be too liberal to the lawyers; they will not do the work one bit the better."

Copley took ten days off to make the pilgrimage he had so long delayed to the works of art in Philadelphia. A copy of Titian's *Venus,* he wrote, "is fine in coloring, I think, beyond any picture I have seen," but remembering the lesson West had given him, he added: "I must observe, had I performed that picture, I should have been apprehensive the figures in the background were too strong." He was impressed by a *Holy Family* attributed to Correggio. "The flesh is very plump, soft, and animated, and is possessed of a pleasing richness beyond what I have seen. In short, there is such a flowery luxuriance in that picture as I have seen in no other." On his return to Boston, Copley stopped at New Brunswick, New Jersey, where he saw several portraits attributed to Van Dyck.

While he was in New York, West had notified him that his likeness of Greenwood's mother had been well received, and had again urged him to study abroad before it was too late. "I am still of the same opinion that it will every way answer your expectations, and I hope to see you in London in the course of the year."

At last Copley found the courage to write West that he would come; he would take a fishing vessel to Leghorn, study the old masters in Italy, and then proceed to London. West's reply was enthusiastic, but Copley dallied for more than a year until late in 1773 before he could make himself take the decisive step of engaging passage. That the voyage of America's leading painter to Europe was regarded all over the Colonies as a matter of patriotic importance is shown by the letters of introduction to European notables that were sent him by fellow country-men he had never met, including John Morgan, Philadelphia's famous physician-art-lover.

After years of delay, the Colonial master was poised for flight to Italy, but he did not take off. Perhaps this time he was held back by a political crisis. His wife's family, the Clarkes, had imported some tea. They were to be guests of honor at the Boston Tea Party.

Copley's family ties and personal obligations presented him with a series of plausible reasons for his perpetual postpone-ment of his trip abroad, but we may well wonder if they tell the whole story. Fundamental to his entire professional career was the dichotomy between the style he had worked out for himself in semi-isolation and the art of the world centers which he had read about but never seen. The prestige of those dimly imagined pictures was so great Copley was convinced that, once he met them face to face, he would have to surrender his own identity to theirs. In an esthetic sense, he would have to be born again. Surely some part of the mind of this great work-man did not wish to abandon everything he was, even in ex-change for something better. The creation of the mighty por-traits of his American years must have given him satisfaction; he could not have worked so strongly had he not known, in the profound recesses of his nature, that he was working well.

After the failure of *Mary Warner* had convinced him that he could not imitate foreign art on the basis of the written word, Copley turned his back on Europe. Although his conscious mind may not have recorded the fact, his pictures show us that somewhere deep down he had come to realize that half-measures would not suffice: he must either go abroad or follow his own star. While he dallied in conversation with the first alternative, his painting hand quietly followed the second. For eight long years, he worked with passionate constancy in his homespun manner. These were golden years for his art. By what he regarded as misfortune, he achieved greatness.

Copley's mature American work is characterized by seriousness and intensity. He permits himself no smiles in his paintings, no frivolous passages, even as there are no jokes in his letters. Misunderstanding the conceits and furbelows of the English School, he renders them with a matter-of-factness that carries them into a different intellectual atmosphere. When in his full-length of *Thomas Hancock* (Plate 23) he painted a looped red curtain dangling from nothing and in mid-air, he forced himself to believe it. This may have taken some doing, but it added immeasurably to the power of the canvas.

As his native realism triumphed, increasingly he banished the fancy conceptions of Europe to the rear reaches of his pictures; curtains and urns became dim shapes almost lost in shadow. When about 1760 he had shown Epes Sargent leaning on a column, the incongruous classical symbol had loomed in the foreground. *Thomas Amory,* executed roughly a decade later, is quite similar in composition, yet the column has become so vague we must look twice to be sure it is there. It no longer bears the sitter's weight; now he leans on the cane he carried every day.   (Plates 16 and 21.)

More and more, Copley used light and shadow to focus attention on the parts of the picture he considered important. Amory's face and hands are accentuated with almost brutal strength, while the costume that would have been emphasized by an aristocratic painter is blacked out to a point of esthetic danger. Hardly enough body is shown to hold the picture together.

Copley never dared use this method on the ladies. Often he painted their clothes in great detail, but his interest was clearly less in displaying luxury than in rendering exactly what he saw. Not only did he draw scarf and jewel and dress as if they were bits of still life, but he carried this meticulous, almost scientific approach to other accessories. *Mrs. Ezekial Goldthwait* (Plate 22) contains an exact likeness of an embroidered chair, while the bowl of fruit toward which the sitter stretches her hand is rendered with passionate fidelity. That upon occasion his interest in reality for its own sake induced him to paint still lives independently of portraits is indicated by the inclusion in our nation's first recorded group exhibition—The Columbianum, Philadelphia, 1795—of five such compositions attributed to "Mr. Copley of Boston": four "Fruit Pieces" and "A Wood Duck, still life." There is also a "Portrait in Crayons, by ditto." We cannot be altogether certain that these pictures were actually by his hand, or the work of his American years, since by that time he had been abroad for two decades. Copley was famous, and distinguished names draw to themselves like lodestones the works of less celebrated artists. No still lives that exist today can be attributed to Copley, but he might easily have been drawn to such pictures by his passion for recording nature exactly and with great sincerity.

Copley's sincerity communicates itself to the viewer and is perhaps the psychological basis of his power. It is the naïve earnestness of a primitive. Painting better pictures than any he had ever seen, he was forced to seek his own solutions. Thus he moved naturally in directions dictated by his temperament; he explored regions that interested him, and slighted all others. This process was less likely to produce a suave and rounded style than a narrow, powerful one.

Copley wanted to depict as truthfully as possible the men and women he knew. Although he complained of his fellow citizens because they judged a portrait by its resemblance to the sitter, he shared their attitude. Never did a great painter occupy himself more singleheartedly with what simple people consider the portraitist's sole function: the creation of likenesses. Lacking the technical virtuosity that would have enabled him to reproduce the surface appearance of nature—a young girl's dewy cheek, the glisten of light in her hair—he was forced to dig for something more psychologically profound. Unable to describe, he had to interpret. For this arduous labor, he found that a likeness of the face was not enough; a likeness of the body must be added. He made as much use of pose as feature.

So great was his concentration on personal character that his pictures, if hung beside the works of his European contemporaries, would often seem caricatures. The silversmith Nathaniel Hurd leans toward us informally in a bright dressing gown. Over the gleaming silk there smiles good-naturedly the face of a fat man, shrewd, perhaps brutal, certainly intelligent.

Professor John Winthrop of Harvard (Plate 24) is a frightening rendition of that modern version of a Christian martyr, a scientific fanatic. We know that this astronomer would sacrifice his wife, his children, even himself to a new observation on the transit of Venus. What the wheel was to Catherine, that telescope is to Winthrop. It is the symbol of his martyrdom and the proof of his salvation.

Mrs. Paul Richard (Plate 20) shows us an old lady who is far from beautiful, but could certainly get the best of a Countess by Reynolds when it comes to horse-trading. But we must stop; the list could go on for a hundred pages.

Copley made visible to our eyes a generation, painted profoundly and truthfully, with neither flattery nor criticism. He dwelt on the aspect of humanity that most interested him; on character. Living in a period of great social upheaval, he never editorialized; he tried to ignore political conflicts. Yet the curtain that hung between his quiet studio and the battles of the world was suddenly rent from top to bottom. He was forced to play an important part in the negotiations that led up to the Boston Tea Party and thus precipitated the American Revolution.

FIVE

The Painter and the Tea

COPLEY'S FATHER-IN-LAW, Richard Clarke, was an agent for the East India Company and one of the consignees of the tea whose destruction was to be a turning-point in American history. As soon as their names were published, the agents became the object of patriotic fury. "On the morning of the second instant," Clarke's firm wrote to their London correspondent, "about one o'clock we were roused out of our sleep by a violent knocking at the door of our house, and on looking out of the window we saw (for the moon shone very bright) two men in the courtyard." They presented a letter demanding that Clarke and his sons appear at noon the next day at the Liberty Tree "to make a public resignation of your commission. . . . Fail not, at your peril!"

All the bells in the meeting houses started ringing at eleven o'clock the next morning and continued till twelve; the town crier hurried through the streets summoning the people to the Liberty Tree. In the meantime, the consignees, supported by their male relatives, were huddled in terrified conference in

[58]

Clarke's warehouse; it is quite possible that Copley was among them. They decided to stay where they were "and to endeavor with the assistance of a few friends to oppose the designs of the mob if they should come to offer us any insult or injury."

At noon the bells stopped ringing; the merchants knew the meeting was assembled and waited to see how the popular fury would manifest itself. Finally there was a sound of distant shouting that grew louder until suddenly a mob of several hundred men poured into King Street; they gathered in front of the warehouse and waved a forest of cudgels at the barred windows. After some negotiations, the merchants admitted a committee of nine to the counting room. As spokesman, William Molineaux demanded a promise that the tea be sent back immediately and no duty paid; despite the roar of menacing voices below, the merchants refused. Then the mob stormed the warehouse. By taking the doors off the hinges, they broke into the lower floor, but "some twenty gentlemen" were able to defend the narrow stair to the counting room. Finally the patriot leaders, who had probably intended only to frighten the merchants, pulled the mob off. Shouting and singing, the brawny apprentices and dock workers disappeared down King Street.

That was only the beginning. When night fell, the Clarke family received another threatening message. A letter of Henry Pelham's thus described the state of Boston: "The various discordant noises with which my ears are continually assailed in the day, passing of carts and a constant throng of people, the shouting of an undisciplined rabble, the ringing of bells, the sounding of horns in the night when it might be expected that an universal silence should reign, and all nature, weary with the toils of day, should be composed to rest, but instead of that nothing but a confused medley of the rattling of carriages, the noises of pope-drums, and the infernal yell of those who are fighting for the possessions of the devil."

On the morning of November 17, 1773, Richard Clarke's family assembled at his house to welcome a brother who had just returned from Europe; Copley was probably present, for it was an important family jubilation. "All at once," a letter to Clarke's London correspondents reveals, "the inmates of the dwelling were startled by a violent beating at the door, accompanied with shouts and the blowing of horns, creating considerable alarm. The ladies were hastily bestowed to places of safety, while the gentlemen secured the avenues from the lower story as well as they were able. The yard and the vicinity were soon filled with people." If Copley was there, he saw the nightmare that had haunted his childhood come true at last; the waterfront mob, the drunken stevedores, the sadistic bullies, had gathered to overwhelm him.

"One of the inmates [of the house]," the letter continues, "warned them from an upper story to disperse, but, getting no other reply than a shower of stones, he discharged a pistol. Then came a shower of missiles that broke in the lower windows and damaged some of the furniture." A bloody battle seemed at hand, but at that instant some Whig leaders came galloping into the courtyard. They gathered the mob together, harangued them for a moment, and then led them down the street. Foiled of their prey, the rioters shouted over their shoulders threats for the future.

Here was a situation which every nerve in the body of the pacifist painter wished to flee. Having no interest in politics, wishing only to pursue his calling in peace, he had remained non-partisan, friendly with Hancock and Adams though a son-in-law of Clarke. But his long record of taking no sides made him the perfect person to represent the merchants in their negotiations with the patriots. When all the consignees of the tea found it expedient to flee to Castle William, the fortress in the bay guarded by British troops, Copley became their agent in Boston.

He was glad to do so, for he was moved by more than family piety; opposed to violence to the very core of his being, he was horrified by the turbulent path down which American politics was slipping; he knew that at the end of that path lay civil war. Since it is customary for American patriotic historians who wish to glorify the Revolution to classify as Tories all those who were not in favor of extreme measures, Copley is often referred to as "the Tory painter." Many writers have explained that his economic interest lay that way, since almost all his sitters were Tories; actually his sitters were divided about equally between the two sides. He had friends on both sides. Since his own background was Whig and his wife's was Tory, he saw there was right on both sides. He realized that the English commercial laws were oppressive, but he felt their repeal could be secured by peaceful means. More clear-sighted than most, he saw the fallacy in the belief of many peace-loving Colonials that violence can be turned on and off like a tap; that Parliament could be frightened into relaxing its laws and harmony be re-established. With the insight of a quiet man who hated all brutality, he perceived that force breeds force. He saw both parties entrenching themselves into stubborn positions that could not be abandoned. He knew that if angry measures were taken to destroy the tea, compromise would no longer be possible, and knowing this, he performed what was for a man of his temperament an act of heroism: he threw himself into the fray and tried to beat down the swords of the antagonists.

Tightening his shrinking nerves to the point of action, he called on Adams, Hancock, and Doctor Warren; he argued that a violent solution of the problem of the tea would bring with it a train of calamities whose end could not be foreseen. Did he know that these men understood what he understood, that they really wanted a war of independence despite the suaveness with which they phrased their desire for ultimate compromise? Probably not. In 1775, after the hostilities had started in earnest, Copley wrote to his wife: "How warmly I expostulated with some of the violent Sons of Liberty against their proceedings they must remember, and with how little judgment, in their opinion, did I then seem to speak."

When talking to the leaders failed, the timid painter forced himself to appear before town meetings. The day after the tea arrived, the patriots assembled in Old South Church to determine on action; Copley argued eloquently for moderation. Yet the meeting voted that the tea must be returned without any duty being paid, although this would have ruined the merchants whose ships, according to the English law, would have been subject to confiscation. Copley then secured an adjournment to give him time to consult with the consignees. These gentlemen, safe behind the battlements of Castle William, were no more eager for compromise than the patriots; they sent Copley back with a flat refusal to make any concessions. His heart heavy, he carried their letter across the channel; he wandered up and down the waterfront in hesitation, past the dark corners that had terrified his childhood but that now he rarely saw.

Perhaps that evening he was not conscious where his feet had strayed, for he knew that the lives of thousands of men lay wrapped up in the paper in his pocket. It was Pandora's box; once opened in a full town meeting of Boston patriots, it would loose he shrank to think what calamities of civil war.

For a long time he paced with the slow steps of deliberation, but suddenly his footfalls were rapid in the stillness. He hurried to the slip and took a boat back to Castle William. "Mr. Copley," the Clarkes wrote their London correspondents, "on his return to town, fearing the most dreadful consequences, thought best not to deliver our letter to the selectmen, but returned to us at night, representing this." He managed to persuade the partners to promise that they would store the tea until they received instructions from London.

After Copley had presented this compromise proposal to the meeting the next morning, the patriot orators expressed great indignation and flayed the consignees, while the crowd cheered and shouted threats. Copley seemed to be the only silent man in the meeting. Finally he pressed his white lips together, and rose to ask for the floor. A sudden stillness fell while all turned to see what the devil's advocate would suggest. If he could prevail on the Clarkes to appear, he asked, could he be assured that they would be "treated with civility while in the meeting . . . and their persons be safe till their return to the place from whence they should come?" The matter was put to a vote, and the Clarkes' safety assured unanimously. Copley then moved that he be given two hours. The motion was passed and the meeting temporarily adjourned.

Copley set out for Castle William with a slightly lighter heart; himself a disciple of peace, he was convinced that if only the adversaries could meet and talk together, they would see that both sides were made up of human beings; they would come to a compromise. It was blowing hard when he stepped into the boat that was to bear him to the castle, but the man who feared the sea was too full of the importance of his mission to be afraid. Perhaps if he could muster his arguments well enough, he could prevent civil war. The consignees, however, were less idealistic than he; they preferred to remain behind the fortifications of the castle.

Copley argued for so long that he was very late in returning to the meeting. As he walked dejectedly down the empty street to Old South Church, he could hear the emotional soaring of an orator's voice, followed, as the voice rose in a crescendo, by a roar from the crowd. He knew that his having kept the patriots waiting had not improved their tempers. The timid painter, we may be sure, hesitated for a moment at the door before he took a deep breath and went in.

The orator in the pulpit stopped in the middle of a sentence; there was a mighty rustling as almost a thousand men turned in their seats. Copley's measured steps took him to the front of the hall, but his voice was dry and thin on the first few words he spoke. He said, according to the minutes of the meeting, "that he had been obliged to go to the castle. He hoped that if he had exceeded the time allowed him, they would consider the difficulty of the passage by water at this season as an apology." A dead silence greeted these words; everyone was wondering why Copley had returned alone.

That night Copley described in a letter to his brother-in-law how he had argued, with all the eloquence he could muster, that the consignees had refused to appear, not from fear of being attacked, but because they felt that their presence would only further enrage the meeting if they did not do what the meeting wanted. Their opposition to the patriots' demands, he insisted, was due not to "obstinacy and unfriendliness to the community, but rather to the necessity to discharge a trust, a failure in which would ruin their reputations as merchants, and their friends who had put large sums of money in the enterprise. . . . I further observed you had shown no disposition to bring the tea into the town, nor would you; but only must be excused from being the active instruments in sending it back." He had assured the patriots that this promise would enable them to achieve their ends by peaceful means, since if the tea remained unloaded the captains of the boats would eventually have to take it back on their own initiative.

"In short," Copley continued, "I have done every possible thing, and although there was a unanimous vote passed declaring this unsatisfactory, yet it cooled the resentment and they dissolved without doing or saying anything that showed an ill-temper to you." Fifteen days later, however, the patriots dressed themselves as Mohawks and threw the tea into the bay, lighting, despite Copley's best efforts, the fuse that was to detonate the American Revolution.

The only result of Copley's intervention was to make him an object of suspicion to the more rabid patriots; as Henry Pelham complained in his letters, anyone not in favor of violence was branded an enemy of liberty. During April, 1774, the painter entertained Colonel George Watson, a British mandamus commissioner. He wrote to his brother-in-law that at about midnight, some hours after Watson had left, "a number of persons came to the house, knocked at the front door, and awoke Sukey [his wife] and myself. I immediately opened the window and asked them what they wanted. They asked if Mr. Watson was in the house. I told them he was not. They made some scruples of believing me, and asked if I would give them my word and honor that he was not in the house. I replied: 'Yes.' They said he had been here, and desired to know where he was. I told them . . . he was gone, and I supposed out of town. . . . They then desired to know how I came to entertain such a rogue and villain."

Copley tried to placate the growing mob by telling them that Watson had been to see Hancock earlier in the day; in any case, he had left. The rioters seemed satisfied and went off up the street, but they were soon back, milling under his window and giving the "Indian yell." Copley leaned out and said he thought he had convinced them Watson was not there. "They said they could take no man's word," the painter's letter continues. "They believed he was here, and if he was they would know it, and my blood would be on my own head if I had deceived them, or if I entertained him or any such villain for the future." After much more talk between the timid artist at the window and the brawny men below, a chaise with the curtains down came galloping up. Its mysterious occupant called over the leaders, conferred with them for a minute or two, and then the chaise moved off with the crowd following behind in a tight, grumbling mass. The street became as quiet as it had been in those now almost unbelievable years before Americans had grown to hate each other.

Copley was deeply shaken. "What a spirit!" he wrote. "What if Mr. Watson had stayed, as I had pressed him to, to spend the night! I must either have given up a friend to the insult of a mob, or had my house pulled down or perhaps my family murdered.''

SIX

The Traveled Road

IT IS A STRANGE FACT that some three weeks after the mob had threatened his house and family, Copley set out for his long-delayed trip to Europe, leaving behind in faction-torn Boston his invalid mother, his half-brother, his wife and four small children. He had put off his transatlantic studies for years, waiting for a propitious time; why did he pick this time that of all times seems the most unpropitious? Perhaps he felt that it was a matter of now or never. He foresaw civil strife, but his letters home make it clear that he did not expect major trouble to come as soon as it did. Perhaps he hoped to rush through his studies in Italy, and be in a position to support his wife and children in England by the time the Revolution started. However modern writers may fulminate in the name of patriotism to a nation then non-existent, it did not seem treason to Copley to flee a civil war he thought unnecessary by going to the capital of the nation of which he had always been a subject.

Copley must have sailed with a heavy heart. Not only was he leaving his family at a difficult time, but he was embarking to face terrors from which he had shrunk for years: an ocean voyage, life among strangers, the roads of Europe which he believed crawled with bandits waiting to cut his throat. So dark were his anticipations that the reality he found seemed almost unbelievably rosy; his letters from England are cheerful in the extreme. He was amazed at the genteelness of the public coaches and the inn; at the beauty of the women that was "almost enough to warm a statue and bring it to life."

The retiring painter, who had never gone out of his way to be friendly to strangers, was deeply impressed by the courtesy with which he was received in London. "There is a great deal of manly politeness in the English," he wrote. West invited him to come to dinner every evening when he was not otherwise engaged, introduced him to Reynolds, and took him to the Royal Academy, where the Bostonian, used to the prudery at home, was surprised to find that "the students had a naked model from which they were drawing." Starved so long for good artistic talk, he plunged into endless discussions with his English colleagues; the thirty-six-year-old Colonial, who had painted immortal pictures, asked questions that a modern art student would hardly deign to answer.

Copley had always wondered how one planned compositions containing groups of figures. Once he had outlived the youthful naïveté that had encouraged him to attempt anything, he had never shown three or more persons in a single picture. Indeed, for the years between 1758 or thereabouts and 1773 he had limited himself to single portraits, not even venturing to place a baby in its mother's arms. Then, just as his American career was closing, he made two attempts at showing a husband and wife together on the same canvas. *Mr. and Mrs. Isaac*

Winslow was only partly successful. The heads, painted in large, reveal Copley's usual shrewd realism, but he did not leave enough space for the bodies. Mr. Winslow, that leading Tory, is shown as a dwarf. However, the other matrimonial brace, *Mr. and Mrs. Thomas Mifflin* (Plate 4), is one of Copley's masterpieces. Using an upright canvas, he gave his sitters plenty of leg room, and he lighted the faces and bodies against a dark background to achieve harmony in space, color, design.

Had Copley stayed in America, he would undoubtedly have worked out the composing of group pictures, as he had worked out so many problems, by the laborious but profound method of personal experimentation. Now a quicker way out offered: he asked more experienced painters. They told him that before you touched brush to canvas, you should make drawings, an expedient almost unknown in America. "The means by which composition is obtained," he wrote Henry Pelham, is "easier than I thought it had been. The sketches are made from life, not only from figures singly but often by groups. This, you remember, we often talked of, and by this a great difficulty is removed that lay on my mind."

For all the courtesy with which he was received, Copley felt timid and strange. He was glad to stay with other Colonials at the New England Coffee House, and one of the most ecstatic passages in his letters describes a dinner at the home of Thomas Hutchinson, the royal governor of Massachusetts, who had shortly before found Boston too hot to hold him. "There were twelve of us together, all Bostonians, and we had choice salt fish for dinner."

When Copley left for the Continent after six weeks in London, he was delighted to go with George Carter, an English painter who he hoped would protect him in the terrifying mazes of Europe. "Mr. Carter," he wrote to his mother, "[is] well versed in traveling, has the languages, both Italian and French. This makes very convenient and agreeable. He is a very polite and sensible man who has seen much of the world. It is most probably one house will hold us both at Rome, and the same coach bring us back to England."

However, Copley leaned too heavily on his new friend, for he did not find France to his liking. Although the scenery was picturesque, "the victuals were so badly dressed that even Frenchmen complained of it. . . . You must know those French wines are not as strong as our cider." In Paris, a week's stay enabled him to see "all that is worth seeing." He took elaborate notes on Rubens's coloring for the instruction of Henry Pelham, but he wrote: "I think the pictures are very unequal in merit." As for "the works of Raphael, Correggio, Titian, Guido, etc.," he hoped "I have not seen their most perfect works." To a man from a desert island, whose dreams of women have been inspired by romantic books, even the most beautiful sirens would certainly be disappointing.

Copley's continual complaining eventually annoyed Carter. "Sir," he said, "we are now more than eight hundred miles from home, through all which way you have not had a single care that I could alleviate. I have taken as much pains as to the mode of conveying you as if you had been my wife, and I cannot help telling you that she, though a delicate little woman, accommodated her feelings to her situation with more temper than you have done."

Carter's diary is full of such irritated references to Copley. "This companion of mine is rather a singular character. He seems happy at taking things at the wrong end, and labored near a half-hour today to prove that a huckaback towel was softer than a Barcelona silk handkerchief. . . .

"My agreeable companion suspects he has got a cold upon his lungs. He is now sitting by a fire, the heat of which makes me very faint, a silk handkerchief about his head and a white pocket one about his neck, applying fresh fuel and complaining that the wood of this country don't give half the heat that the wood of America does; and has just finished a long-winded discourse upon the merits of an American wood fire to one of our coal. He had never asked me yet, and we have been up an hour, how I do or how I passed the night; 'tis an engaging creature."

Carter continually teased Copley because he knew no language but English, and the two men quarreled like children about the merits of their respective countries. Sarcastically, Carter describes Copley holding forth on the future of America, insisting that in less than a hundred years it would have an independent government, and that "the woods will be cleared, and lying in the same latitude, they shall have the same air as in the South of France. Art would then be encouraged there and great artists arrive."

Here is Copley's traveling costume as Carter described it: "He had on one of those white French bonnets which, turned on one side, admit of being pulled over the ears; under this was a yellow and red silk handkerchief, with a large Catherine-wheel flambeaued upon it, such as may be seen upon the necks of those delicate ladies who cry Malton oysters—this flowed halfway down his back. He wore a red-brown or rather cinnamon greatcoat with a friar's cape, and worsted binding of a yellowish white; it hung near his heels, out of which peeped his boots.

Under his arm he carried the sword which he bought in Paris [for protection against bandits, we may be sure], and a hickory stick with an ivory head. Joined to this dress, he was very thin, pale, a little pock-marked, prominent eyebrows, small eyes which after fatigue seemed a day's march in his head."

Copley soon lost his high opinion of his companion. "He was," the Colonial wrote, "a sort of snail which crawled over a man in his sleep, and left its slime and no more."

From Genoa, the last major stop before he reached Rome, Copley poured out his loneliness and ambition to his wife: "I am happy to be so near the end of my journey. Though not fatigued, I am impatient to get to work, and to try if my hand and my head cannot do something like what others have done, by which they have astonished the world and immortalized themselves, and for which they will be admired as long as this earth shall continue." But he was afraid that his art would separate him from his family. "As soon as possible, you shall know what my prospects are in England, and then you will be able to determine whether it is best for you to go there or for me to return to America. It is unpleasant to leave our dear connexions; but if in three of four years [in England] I can make as much as will render the rest of our life easy, and leave something to our family if I should be called away, I believe you would think it best [for me] to spend that time there. Should this be done, be assured I am ready to promise you that I will go back and enjoy that domestic happiness which our little farm is so capable of affording."

But the thought of spending three or four years away from home overwhelmed him with emotion. "Although the connexion of man and wife as man and wife may have an end, yet that of love, which is pure and heavenly, may be perfected. Not that my love is not as perfect as it can be in the present state, but we may be capable of loving more by being more conformed to the infinite source of love. I am anxious lest you suffer by my absence."

In Rome, Copley rushed to the galleries, stared for hours at the paintings of the old masters, and then tried immediately to put his new technical discoveries down on canvas. All his life he had believed that greatness existed only in Europe and the past. Faced at last with the pictures about whose glories he had read, he had no more interest in the technique he had laboriously worked out for himself during long years of isolation; the style that was to make him immortal seemed now worthless. He preferred to imitate the Carracci and Raphael. And he adhered to this determination, although he continued to be a little disappointed by the old masters. He wrote to Pelham that the difference between Titian and Raphael and the common run of painters was not so great as he had been led to suppose by the fame they enjoyed.

The first picture he painted in Italy, a double portrait of Mr. and Mrs. Ralph Izard (Plate 30), reveals a confused state of mind. The two faces are painted with much of the hard, strong draftsmanship he brought with him from America, but Mrs. Izard's cheeks are a rich and artificial red. The whole picture gleams more brightly than his Boston canvases, yet the color is not organic; it seems to have been applied from the outside. Copley had often defined his sitters' environments by the use of details: an upholstered chair, a pen, a tool. The Izards' environment was Rome, and in his fascination with that fabled city Copley widened the canvas to include the following objects: an antique Greek vase,[1] a classic column, a richly embroidered curtain, some heavily carved furniture in the latest Italian mode, the statue of Orestes and Electra he had seen in the National Museum, and the Colosseum done in chocolate color. He wanted to get everything in at once.

Pleased with the result, he painted *The Ascension*. (Plate 25.) This being his first complicated composition and his first religious painting, he was able almost completely to cast off his American moorings. The result is an amazingly successful picture which has always been underestimated as a work of art because it is so clearly in the manner of Raphael. Copley showed tremendous skill as an imitator; had he wished, he could undoubtedly have been one of the greatest forgers of all time.

A line of figures in attitudes of adoration and surprise are placed before a softly indicated green landscape. Their robes are gems of brilliant color: dark green, red, emerald blue. The squatness of their bodies ties them to the earth in contrast with the tall and high-flying Christ who rises in a swirl of yellow cloud. The picture bristles with the forest of gestures so dearly beloved by the "historical painters," but perhaps because the canvas is small—a little less than three feet by a little more than two—they are unobtrusive. Christ is ascending—you cannot in your imagination pull him down—and the figure doubled up with emotion in the foreground could not be straightened out by a two-ox team.

[1] How faithfully Copley adhered to the portrait approach in the painting of accessories is revealed by the following quotation from the archeologist William B. Dinsmoor: "This vase, though now lost, was so accurately delineated by Copley that modern archeologists have been able to identify it just as satisfactorily as if it still existed, as a work by, or at least in the manner of, the so-called 'Niobid Painter' of about 450 B.C."

Copley wrote home that Gavin Hamilton, who shared with West the leadership of the English neo-classical school, had examined the picture. He was "lavish in its praises, and he says he never saw a finer composition in his life, and that he knows no one who can equal it." Copley determined then and there to set up as an historical as well as a portrait painter. He confided to Pelham that Hamilton had told him he was better equipped than West, since he could do portraits as well as history.

Copley was now enamored by the vision of a successful English career. When his wife wrote to him that Boston, occupied by five British regiments, had become highly unpleasant, he replied: "I find you will not regret leaving Boston; I am sorry it has become so disagreeable. I think this will determine me to stay in England. . . . But to give you the trouble of crossing the sea with the children makes me very anxious."

SEVEN

One Common Ruin

SOON COPLEY had more cause for anxiety; late in September, 1774, he read in a London paper that British battleships were bombarding Boston. Although the report was contradicted in the same paper, he was very worried, nor could he set his mind at rest till he received a letter from his wife a month later.

He now arranged to get London papers by every post—once or twice a week—and when they arrived, he picked them up "with trepidation." He wrote to Pelham: "Could anything be more fortunate than the time of my leaving Boston? Poor America. I hope for the best, but I fear the worst. Yet certain I am she will finally emerge from her present calamity and become a mighty empire. And it is a pleasing reflection that I shall stand amongst the first of the artists that shall have led the country to the knowledge and cultivation of the fine arts, happy in the pleasing reflection that they will one day shine with a luster not inferior to what they have done in Greece and Rome." In the same letter, he expressed his determination to settle in London. Had he left Boston before he did, he was to

[77]

explain, "it would have done more violence to myself and dear wife to have fixed in England. But now there is no choice left."

In June, 1775, he left for Parma to copy Correggio's *Saint Jerome*. No sooner had he arrived than he received a letter written by Greenwood from London saying that civil war had started in America, and that some two hundred people had been killed already. Frantically, Copley tried to find some English papers, but none were to be had. All he could learn was rumor, and that became increasingly alarming. "I have seen a letter from Rome," he wrote to his mother, "by which [I] find mention is made of a skirmish having been at Lexington, and that numbers were killed on both sides. I am exceedingly uneasy, not knowing to what you may be exposed in the country that is now become the seat of war. This is the evil I greatly dreaded while I was in America. Sure I am the breach cannot now be healed, and that [the] country will be torn in pieces, first by the quarrel with Great Britain until it is a distinct government, and then with civil discord till time has settled it into some permanent form of government. What that will be no man can tell. Whether it will be free or despotic is beyond the reach of human wisdom to decide."

When a letter came from Pelham, it was not reassuring. "Alas! my dear brother, where shall I find words sufficiently expressive of the distractions and distresses of this once flourishing and happy people. . . . My hand trembles when I inform you that [the] sword of civil war is now unsheathed." Pelham, whose sympathies were Tory, then described the battle of Lexington quite differently from the descriptions we find in American textbooks. The British "regulars made a retreat that does honor to the bravest and most disciplined troops that ever Europe bred. The fatigues and conduct of this little army is not to be paralleled in history. They marched that day not less than fifty miles, were constantly under arms—part of them, at least— from ten o'clock at night till an hour after sunset the next evening, the whole of the time without any refreshment, attacked by an enemy they could not see, for they skulked behind trees, stone walls, etc., and surrounded by not less than ten thousand men, who most vigorously assaulted them with fresh men. In short, considering the circumstances, it was almost a miracle they were not entirely destroyed. When the battle ended, they had not near a charge a man."

Since then Boston, which had remained in the possession of the British, had been besieged and blockaded by the patriots. "It is inconceivable the distress and ruin this unnatural dispute has caused this town and its inhabitants. Almost every shop and store is shut. No business of any kind going on. You will here wish to know how it is with me. I can only say that I am with the multitudes rendered very unhappy; the little I have collected entirely lost. The clothes upon my back and a few dollars in my pocket are now the only property which I have the least command of. What is due me, I can't get, and I have now a hundred guineas' worth of business begun which will never afford me a hundred farthings."

This news was bad enough, but Copley was terrified lest he hear worse. "It may be," he wrote to his Tory half-brother, "for my fears suggest many terrible things, that you are called to arm yourself. But if you should be, it is my injunction that you do not comply with such a requisition, if this does not come too late, which I pray God it may not. . . . I have this exceedingly at heart and trust you will implicitly oblige me in this way. I conjure you to do as I desire! For God's sake, don't think this a trifling thing! My reasons are very important. You must follow my directions, and be neuter at all events."

Copley wrote letter after letter to his wife, urging her to leave Boston with the children at once. "I should fly to you, but the distance is too great. . . . I find there is a great deal of work in the picture I am copying. My anxiety almost renders me incapable of proceeding with it, but it must be done." Communication was so interrupted that he did not learn that his wife had sailed until he received word of her safe arrival in London. "My thoughts are constantly on you and our children," he wrote her. "You tell me you brought three, but do not say which you left behind. I suppose it was the youngest, he being too delicate to bring." Copley had guessed right; it was the youngest, who was soon to die in beleaguered Boston.

When Copley heard that Henry Pelham had stayed behind because their aged mother was afraid to make the arduous trip across the ocean, he wrote him long and eloquent letters, pointing out the danger of remaining. The English, he insisted, would "pursue determined methods" because they "so resent the outrage offered to them in the destruction of the tea." If only the patriot leaders had taken his advice! But now it was too late for anyone to retract. Although the Americans would win after many years, "oceans of blood will be shed . . . the different towns will have at different times to encounter all the miseries of war, sword, famine, perhaps pestilence." The only thing to do was to flee while there was yet time.

Pelham's letters confirmed his melancholy prophecies. "Mrs. Copley desired we would write a word when we met with fresh meat. You will form some idea of our present disagreeable situation when I tell you that last Monday I eat at General Howe's table at Charlestown Camp the only bit of fresh meat I have tasted for very near four months past. And then not with a good conscience, considering the many persons who in sickness are wanting that and most of the conveniency of life."

Two months later, he summed up the state of mind of the thousands of peaceful folk whose emotions rarely find their way into history books. "Civil war with all its horrors now blasts every tender connexion, every social tie upon which the happiness of mankind so materially depends. We are now unhappily afloat in one common ruin, and have only left us the mortifying remembrances of those halcyon days of ease and peace which we now in vain wish to re-enjoy."

"We still continue in the same state . . ." he wrote from Boston during January, 1776. "Both sides strengthening their works, and preventing the other from receiving supplies. Pork and peas, and little enough of that, still continues to be our diet; a baked rice pudding without butter, milk, or eggs; or a little salt fish without butter, we think luxurious living. Lamenting our most disagreeable situation is the only theme of our discourse. Contriving ways and means to get a pound of butter, a quart of peas, to eat; or three or four rotten boards, the ruins of some old barn, to burn, our only business; and the recollection of having some friends at a distance from this scene of anarchy and confusion almost our only happiness. . . .

"I don't think if I had liberty I could find the way to Cambridge, though I am so well acquainted with the road. Not a hillock six feet high but what is entrenched, not a pass where a man could go but what is defended by cannon. Fences pulled down, houses removed, woods grubbed up, fields cut into trenches and moulded into ramparts, are but a part of the changes the country has gone through."

Doggedly Copley finished his copy of the Correggio and, although his heart must have burned to join his exiled wife in London, he continued the journey that was to prepare him to make his living in that sophisticated city. He went to Mantua, Venice, Innsbruck, Augsburg, Stuttgart, Mannheim, Coblenz, Cologne, Düsseldorf, Utrecht, Amsterdam, Leiden, Rotterdam, Antwerp, Brussels, Ghent, Bruges, Lille, and then hurried through Paris to London, arriving late in 1775.

It was a great joy to embrace his wife and children, but the reunited family could find no high spirits with which to face the future in the strange and difficult city to which they had fled. Most of their relations and friends, all the world they had ever known, were menaced and racked by civil war. "As to England," Mrs. Copley wrote to Henry Pelham, "you must not expect from me any account of it at present, for my thoughts are so intent upon America that at times I can scarcely realize myself to be out of it. I have not had the least inclination to visit any of the public places of entertainment, . . . for I think we are so made for each other that we cannot be happy when we have reason to think our friends are exposed to distress. . . . Every account increases my distress. I pray heaven to prepare me for all events!"

EIGHT

An Old Dog and New Tricks

THE STRAIN gradually lessened, for by the time Washington occupied Boston, all of Copley's close relatives had found refuge in British possessions; yet the environment in which he moved was hardly cheering. Like many an American after him, the painter discovered that the English, who had received him so politely when he was a stranger, were not eager to make him a friend. Although not at heart a Tory, he was forced to rely on the society of the Tory refugees. He attended the weekly dinners of the Loyalist Club, where talk ran drearily on war and poverty; the *émigrés,* whose American property had been confiscated, complained of empty purses with all the ardor of the new poor. Copley was able to join in the chorus, for his savings were tied up in Boston real estate and his painting brought in little money. Although he was elected an associate of the Royal Academy over twenty other candidates, although Benjamin West used all his vast influence to get him commissions, he made so little that his impoverished father-in-law had to help in his support.

[83]

Copley soon found himself in a mood where even slight mishaps seemed overwhelming. To cut short his Roman stay, he had bought casts of the most important antique statues to study in London. They were so badly packed, however, that they arrived in fragments, a misfortune which, his son tells us, "he never ceased to regret during the whole course of his after life."

Copley mourned the casts that were to smooth out the roughness of his Colonial technique with increasing intensity, for his lack of immediate success in England further convinced him that he must abandon the crudely honest approach he had worked out for himself in isolation and must learn to paint like fashionable British artists. This was not easy to achieve. His conscious mind, although guided by newly learned intellectual conceptions, floundered in a deep sea of old habits and instincts. The habits, the result of twenty years of professional practice in the Colonies, were stubborn, but they could be broken; the instincts made the worst trouble. For Copley had been formed by his Colonial environment as surely as a tree is shaped by the soil in which it grows. He could rent a house in the right part of London, he could frequent a good English tailor, he could even amend the crudities of his Yankee speech; but in the profounder recesses of his mind a bright American sun burnt away the mists that softened the English air. He could not help seeing things the wrong way.

The first major picture he painted in London was very strange for its place and time; perhaps he would not have undertaken it had he realized how strange. He had made the acquaintance of Brook Watson, a man who had spent much time in America. That this able and plausible merchant was considered a spy in the British employ and greatly hated by the

American revolutionaries Copley did not know or care. What concerned him was Watson's wooden leg. Its flesh-and-blood predecessor had been bitten off by a shark in Havana Harbor. Watson's description of this catastrophe appealed strongly to the imagination of the painter who had always feared the sea.

When Watson commissioned him to record the bloodcurdling scene in paint, Copley set about the task with great passion and enthusiasm. First he undertook a maneuver unknown to his American practice; he made a series of drawings on gray paper in black chalk heightened with white. He imagined single figures, then combined them. The final drawing was ruled off into squares and transferred to a small canvas on which he painted so elaborate a sketch in oils that it was, in fact, a small version of the finished picture. Then, at long last, he enlarged the sketch into the composition that was shown the public. He was to build up all his major English pictures in such a methodical manner.

Brook Watson and the Shark (Plate 8) is composed on three levels. In the background we see a quay partly hidden by a moored ship; a channel, and a headland with its lighthouse. Dim in the distance, these are surmounted by a misty sky which the sun has turned to yellow. The effect of atmosphere, however, is not carried to the other planes of the picture; not even air separates us from that bloody action. The middle of the canvas is filled with a writhing, horrible shape which separates itself on a second glance into a boat filled far past overflowing with men who gesture in anguish toward the part of the picture nearest to us. There, in the bottom strip, we see a naked man being attacked by a shark.

As Copley painted this nightmare which appealed so profoundly to his own fears, he forgot many of the new tricks he had so expensively learned. The figures, although in violent action, are painted with the wooden, halting solidity of his American years; the colors—cold yellows and greens and blues —have no superimposed sheen of brightness.

Copley would undoubtedly have been one of the most surprised men in all London if he had been told that the scholars of the future would regard this picture as a landmark in the world evolution of styles. When it was painted in 1778, Reynolds was still president of the Royal Academy and Doctor Johnson's dicta still typified correct British taste. From the point of view of the neo-classicism these men preached, *Brook Watson and the Shark* was an uncouth expression of physical emotion, as unsuitable as if the American had danced with war-whoop and tomahawk in the London streets. Proper neo-classical pictures dealt with the past rather than contemporary scenes; their protagonists were historical heroes; their tragedy was constructed to demonstrate some intellectual conception like patriotism, bravery, or filial piety. To show the bloody personal misfortune of an unimportant contemporary being struck by an evil fate that presented no possibility for moralizing or sentiment: this was revolution. Indeed, the picture was more than a generation before its time; it foreshadowed the work of the French romantic painters who were years later considered great innovators when they produced similar compositions. Géricault's epoch-making *Raft of the Medusa* (1819) is so close to *Brook Watson* in subject matter and conception that some critics believe that the French artist must have been influenced by an engraving after the American's picture.

When Copley exhibited the painting at the Royal Academy, he did not use Watson's name in the title. Yet his contemporaries were so used to another kind of historical painting that they failed to realize that the protagonist had been selected not because of his own importance but to represent humanity as a whole. The Whigs, who hated Brook Watson, accused Copley of painting propaganda in his favor. John Wilkes wrote a poem in which he congratulated the "luckless wight" on having lost only a leg, for, if the shark had bitten at the other end,

> The best of workmen and the best of wood
> Could scarce have made a head as good.

Although *Brook Watson and the Shark* was so successful that Copley sold several replicas, he abandoned the direction of highly romantic painting to turn to a less daring kind of innovation. His next major canvas was a further development of the style which had been pioneered in London a decade before by Benjamin West. Also touched by the American forests, West had broken with the neo-classical canons of historical painting to give the mode a new immediacy. It had long been conventional to paint patriotic homilies based on the death of heroes, but all the most admired critics and artists believed that such scenes were not art unless the protagonists were dressed in classical togas or at least in the neutral and amorphous drapery of Raphael. During 1771, West announced that he intended to paint an event from the siege of Quebec, the *Death of Wolfe*, as realistically as he was able. Although lesser artists had made similar attempts, the connoisseurs were shocked that a major painter should depict modern heroes in the costumes they had actually worn. But the finished canvas was approved by the King, and became one of the most popular pictures ever created in England, for it tapped the market for news pictures which was generations later to be exploited by such magazines as *Life*. Even the critics backwatered, finding new sanctions for West's realistic approach in the works of the ancients.

The *Death of Wolfe,* with its half-naked Indian in the foreground, was removed from the humdrum of everyday London by its exotic setting on the Plains of Abraham. But in 1778, a dramatic happening that screamed for the painter's brush took place at home. The elder Pitt, the Earl of Chatham, suffered, while addressing the House of Lords, a stroke from which he never recovered. Both West and Copley started pictures of this scene that interested every Englishman. "Mr. West," Horace Walpole wrote, "made a small sketch of the death of Lord Chatham, much better expressed and disposed than Copley's. It has none but the principal persons present; Copley's almost the whole of the peerage, of whom seldom so many are there at once, and in Copley's most are mere spectators. But the great merit of West's is the principal figure, which has his crutch and gouty stockings, which express his feelings and account for his death. West would not finish it not to interfere with his friend Copley."

Since Pitt's seizure had occurred in the presence of many local people and in a building which Londoners passed every day, the interest of Copley's picture had to be based, not on surprise, but recognition. With the literal-mindedness that had been the glory of his American career, he painted from life likenesses of a horde of peers. These he gathered together into a vast, melodramatic group portrait of the House of Lords.   (Plate 7.)

Dressed in state robes of ermine and scarlet, more than fifty noblemen are gathered around the Prime Minister, who has just fallen over backward into the arms of his son. The canvas holds together amazingly well, considering the number of individuals included, but it was impossible to carry a unified emotion through such a horde of faces; the picture seems formal rather than emotional. Yet it is startling in the glow of its color, in its movement, and in the concise sharpness of the myriad portraits. It is polished and finished from ermine to feather, from glossy boot and shoe to glistening buckle and star. The technical brilliance displayed is almost unbelievable when we remember that Copley had been painting in the style only a few years.

In 1781, the members of the Royal Academy looked forward to the crowds which so fine a rendering of so popular a subject would bring to their exhibition, but Copley, who had already refused fifteen hundred guineas for the picture, and had sold subscriptions for twenty-five hundred large engravings, decided it would be profitable to show *The Death of Chatham* by itself and charge admission. Choosing the "Season," when the city was fullest, he scheduled his exhibition at the same time as the Academy's. His fellow artists were so infuriated that they forced his landlord to evict him from the showroom he had rented. When he found another, Sir William Chambers, the famous architect, wrote him their sentiments: "No one wishes Mr. Copley greater success, or is more sensible of his merit, than his humble servant, who, if he may be allowed to give his opinion, thinks no place so proper as the Royal Exhibition to promote either the sale of prints or the raffle for the picture, which he understands are Mr. Copley's motives. Or, if that be objected to, he thinks no place so proper as Mr. Copley's own house, where the idea of a raree-show will not be quite so striking as in any other place, and where his own presence will not fail to be of service to his views."

More than twenty thousand people paid to see Copley's picture, while the receipts of the Royal Academy Exhibition, which contained seven Gainsboroughs and fifteen Reynoldses, fell a third, or more than a thousand pounds, from the previous year. Copley's private show, as the *Morning Post* estimated, made him about five thousand pounds, but it also made him many enemies. When prints of *The Death of Chatham* were completed, it was bruited about that they had been distributed fraudulently, the early impressions not having gone to the early subscribers. All the expert witnesses Copley could bring forth did not entirely silence the rumor.

The merchants, who had worshiped Chatham, flocked to Copley to have their portraits done; he was soon in the full tide of prosperity. He achieved the greatest ambition of a Colonial by becoming a successful painter in the mother city, yet he was not happy. Never a man who made human contacts easily, he found the English stiff and hard to get on with; their manners seemed to him overbearing. Used to being the leading painter of a continent, he felt undervalued in an environment where others had greater reputations than he. He became particularly jealous of the man who had made his English career possible; although he frequented West's studio and seemed as friendly as ever, the keen eye of Hoppner observed that whenever West made a suggestion at a meeting of the Royal Academy, Copley opposed it.

As Copley grew increasingly homesick for Boston, the unending denunciations he heard of the American rebels drove him so far from his non-partisanship in politics that he began to believe the revolution he had once opposed a glorious thing; the former peacemaker became a rabid patriot. When in 1782, he painted the American merchant Elkanah Watson, he resolved to place in the background "a ship bearing to America the acknowledgments of our independence." Such a ship should fly the Stars and Stripes, but the cautious painter was afraid to depict that revolutionary flag lest he offend his other sitters. For a long time the picture stood against the wall unfinished. On December 5, however, he accompanied Watson to the House of Lords to hear the King acknowledge American independence. Sitting there with as non-committal an expression as he could muster, he saw West also in the audience, also holding a vacant look. But when the meeting was over and the King had pronounced, though hesitantly, the fatal words, Copley in great excitement invited Watson to return to his studio. "There," his sitter wrote in his diary, "with a bold hand, a master's touch, and I believe an American heart, he attached to the ship the Stars and Stripes. This, I imagine, was the first American flag hoisted in England."

Copley's historical paintings continued to bring him money and renown. As the London art chronicler Cunningham put it, "No artist was ever more ready than Copley to lend his pencil to passing events." In 1781, Major Pierson, an English officer only twenty-four years old, refused to accept a surrender negotiated by his superiors and, gathering together a group of hot spirits, defeated a French force invading Saint Helier on the Island of Jersey. He was killed at the very moment of victory. No sooner had the news reached England than Copley began mixing paints.

His *Death of Major Pierson* (Plates 6 and 26) is perhaps Copley's masterpiece in the historical style. Everything is color and action. Copley had learned in Italy to break down the rigidity of his American pictures by the use of flowing lines. Although sometimes the method seems facile rather than deeply felt, in this canvas the forms are strong and alive with motion. The artist has been amazingly successful in implying the disorder of war and yet keeping the composition orderly. Too often the men in eighteenth-century battle paintings seem frozen in artificial poses, like the effigies of a waxwork. There is little posing here.

The composition is a conventional neo-classical form borrowed from the stage; a central group slightly back in the picture, and on either side wings of figures that draw the eye inward. Again, however, Copley had made a stylistic departure. On the extreme right we see individuals who have no place at all in that bloody, smoke-filled street. The dying man's wife, a nurse holding his baby, and an older child are fleeing the catastrophe with upraised hands and horror-struck eyes. Copley had broken with the canons of logical versimilitude which the neo-classical theory dictated to bring together episodes whose connections were not historical or physical, but rather emotional. We have here a hint of the multiple images so popular in contemporary art.

Copley, the pacifist, clearly painted the brutal scene from a very personal point of view; it was his own body he saw falling so gracefully down toward oblivion. As models for the fleeing figures, he used his family nurse, his wife, and two of his own children.

Although Copley's pictures now had a fluent look, he had not really become a fluent painter. When the Corporation of London commissioned him to paint *The Repulse of the Floating Batteries at Gibraltar,* he laid out a vast canvas, twenty-five feet by twenty, on which he worked laboriously for six years. A visitor reported that he was literally fighting the battle in his studio, for he had models of the rock, the fortifications, the attacking ships, the guns, and even of the men. These he soberly grouped into the composition he desired. He stood on a platform, and fixed his canvas to rollers so that he could manipulate any part of it within reach of his brush. During 1787, the Corporation of London sent him to Germany, where he painted the portraits of four Hanoverians who had taken part in the defense.

When the picture was finally completed in 1791, he could find no gallery large enough to contain it; he set up a tent in Green Park. But the crowds who flocked to see the structure angered the fashionable residents of Arlington Street, particularly the Duke of Bolton, and Copley was forced to move to another site. Here, however, his huge pavilion obstructed the view of some householders. Copley was forced to move again. He was in despair, until the King came to his rescue, inviting him to put the tent near Buckingham Palace. "*My* wife," he is reported to have said, "won't complain." The royal family attended the opening, and some sixty thousand people followed their example. Again Copley offered competition with a Royal

Academy show, and took away so much business that it was a failure.

Copley alternated portraits with historical paintings. His likenesses were both more various and more uneven than those he had produced in America. Often he had difficulties with his British sitters. Since in Boston amusements had been few, people had been willing to pose for many long hours. Londoners, however, were beckoned by multitudinous diversions. Handling their brushes like fencing foils, English artists amused their sitters by exhibitions of manual dexterity, and finished a face in a few hours. While yet in Boston, Copley had written that his pictures "are almost always good in proportion to the time I give them." But he could no longer match a color to a face on his palette knife; only rarely was he given an opportunity to think deeply. To compete with his rivals, he had to achieve a dash and flare that had been quite foreign to his New England ways.

Under the circumstances, he did remarkably well. His run-of-the-mill English portraits are exemplified by *Augustus Brine*. (Plate 28.) The twelve-year-old boy who strutted into his studio was an aristocrat, the son of a high naval officer and himself already a midshipman in the Royal Navy. Copley hated the supercilious youngster at sight—a bad start for a portrait painter; but he did his best to turn out the picture that was expected of him.

He placed the lad's slim figure quite grandiloquently in a romantic grotto by the side of a turbulent sea. Holding back his blue naval coat with a negligent gesture, the boy lays his hand possessively on a cannon; the cocky expression of the face and the grace of the body express the sitter's complete control of his wild environment.

The spectator's reactions as he studies this canvas develop like a serial story. Your first emotion is irritation, although you are not quite sure what annoys you. Closer study, however, makes annoyance give way to admiration. In the right background Copley painted a stormy sea under a menacing sky. The waves are indicated almost in shorthand by a series of long wavy brushstrokes, but the colors—yellow, blue, brown, and gray—are mingled expertly to give a strong impression of wild water. A ship is sketched in so lightly that you can hardly see it, yet, when you do, you feel the emotions of the invisible mariners who are handling its wind-torn sails. The composition, with its compensating movements of line and form, is suave. Varying chromatically from yellow-buff trousers of a heavy weave to a filmy white collar, the costume, too, is expert in conception and execution. And the face, although more brightly colored than nature, gives a startling impression, not only of aristocratic disdain, but also of the artist's strong feeling of dislike.

"I must have misjudged this portrait," you say to yourself. "It is brilliantly painted." But when you step back again to get a general view, your annoyance returns. Suddenly you realize what is wrong; the picture is fundamentally insincere. The romantic grotto and the boy's pose before it are alien to Copley's temperament. All the superlative ability with which Fate had endowed the painter could not hide his lack of belief in what he was doing.

Others of Copley's sitters were more sympathetic to him than

Midshipman Brine, and of them he made brilliant portraits. His abandonment of the grave, passionate clumsiness of his American years produced a diminution in brute force, but in its place we find a painter-like suavity which is most attractive.

During his trip to Hanover to collect faces of German officers for inclusion in his *Repulse of the Floating Batteries at Gibraltar,* he made a sketch of Colonels Hugo and Schleppengull. (Plate 26.) The two likenesses, although so much more knowing in execution than Copley's Colonial pictures, show that he had not lost his insight into character. He only turned out a completely conventional likeness when some high-born sitter, like Lord Addington, was completely beyond his comprehension. (Plate 29.)

Extending his activity in many directions, Copley painted those family groups, full of people behaving in a normal manner, which are known as conversation pieces. One of these, *The Children of Frances Sitwell,* so impressed the mighty Sitwell clan that, about a century after it was painted, they commissioned another American ex-patriot, John Singer Sargent, to make a companion piece depicting the new brood of children. Osbert Sitwell writes: "Rather unexpectedly, the Copley immediately excited Sargent's admiration, and his first words on seeing it were, 'I can never equal that!' " This is an amusing comment, for *The Sitwell Children,* which is one of Copley's more labored works, shows much of the artificiality for which Sargent's more stilted pictures—including *his* version of the Sitwell children—are criticized. Copley painted much better conversation pieces, including the strong portrait group of his own family and a likeness of George III's daughters, the famous *Three Princesses.* (Frontispiece.)

In some ways, the literalness of Copley's American approach expanded in his new style. When he had wondered how to compose a complicated picture, he had been forced to keep accessories down to a minimum: a merchant would have papers and an inkwell before him; a lady would hold an umbrella or a book. Now, his skill at bringing many things together in a single canvas gave full rein to his bourgeois love of cataloguing objects for their own sake. The three princesses have a dog apiece, and there are two parrots, and a baby buggy, a parasol, and a tambourine.

This profusion annoyed the English artist Hoppner, who wrote, "Is it, Mr. Copley, because you have heard that fine feathers make fine birds that you have concluded that fine clothes will make fine princesses? What a delightful disorder! Why, you have plucked up harmony by the roots and planted confusion in its stead! Princesses, parrots, dogs, grapes, flowers, leaves, are each striving for pre-eminence and opposing with hostile forces all attempts of our wearied eyes to find repose." So spoke the fashionable portraitist. Perhaps he was right on a basis of abstract principles in art, yet it was Copley's gift to commit solecisms and get away with them.

In his book on conversation pieces, Osbert Sitwell's brother, Sacheverell, writes of *The Three Princesses:* "As a picture of children it is pure enchantment. The freshness and liveliness of the young princess at the left is more beautifully rendered than any picture of children by Raeburn, while the baby princess in her wide feathered hat is not less pretty. The three spaniels sport and play in the foreground. . . . Is there any more charming painting of children than this? Their health and vitality overflow into this gay and cheerful design, up to the doves and clusters of grapes twined round the pillars and across the top of the picture. . . . This picture has every quality that should distinguish its English nationality [!] and is, indeed, one of the masterpieces of the English school."

Partly out of misguided patriotism; partly in reaction to an earlier generation of critics who were ashamed of the American vernacular in art; certainly because little distinction has been made between the works of Copley's best London years and his dotage, contemporary Americans tend to undervalue his English pictures. In this activity some English writers are delighted to join, being loath to admit what a major rôle was played by American-born artists in the development of the artistic movement which so influential a critic as Roger Fry believed contained "almost all the painting which creates the spiritual value and importance of the British school." Copley's English portraits cannot compete with Reynolds, Gainsborough, or Raeburn, but in any arenas free of prejudice the best of them could put up a good fight with the best work of such men as Romney and Hoppner. As an "historical painter," Copley undoubtedly was the greatest workman in England. When Reynolds tried to enter this mode, which was then considered a much higher form of art than portraits, he produced compositions which are to Copley's as a flea is to an elephant.

This writer confesses to a personal preference among Copley's canvases for his American portraits. Those burly, dry, downright, painfully executed studies of unadorned Colonial faces have for me a profounder emotional impact than the more sophisticated creations of his later years. But had Copley never painted these pictures, had his reputation been forced to depend entirely on his English work, he would still have had an important place in the world history of art. The old dog had learned new tricks with a skill that showed genius. But it had been a great strain.

NINE

Count No Man Happy

FAME AND PROSPERITY did not keep the artist from becoming increasingly homesick, and when his two youngest children, who had been born in England, died within two weeks of each other during an epidemic of "putrid sore throat," probably diphtheria, his wife received a shock from which she never recovered. From that time on, she, like her husband, walked about their elegant house with a perpetually melancholy face. Wild and meaningless apprehensions scudded through the minds of the nervous pair. Although money was rolling in, the specter of poverty haunted them continually; Copley felt so alien to his English environment that he was sure it would rise up and overwhelm him in the end. Eager to capitalize on the American savings he had invested in his eleven acres of Beacon Hill, he placed them on the market, and in 1795 was delighted to receive an offer of three thousand guineas, about five times what he had paid. Only after he had accepted the offer and a thousand-dollar deposit did he learn that the new State House was to be built on Beacon Hill, and that what he had regarded as farm land would soon become a flourishing part of the city.

Indignantly insisting that he had been defrauded, he sent his young barrister son, John Singleton, Jr., to America to see if he could break the contract. Now that his last tie to America seemed about to be taken from him, Copley felt a wild urge to return to his homeland, to the land where he would again be the most famous of painters, to the land whose social liberty he had grown so passionately to desire. Although his wife dreaded leaving the mild British climate and the greater comfort of their London home, Copley instructed his son to look into the possibility of their returning to America. He gave the boy a letter of introduction to his old opponent, Samuel Adams. The then governor of Massachusetts, whose radicalism made him anathema to the moneyed classes of Boston, must have read with amazement the sentiments of the man who had tried to stop the Revolution, for the painter complimented him on having "borne so distinguished a part in promoting the happiness and the true dignity of his country."

After the younger Copley had arrived in Boston, he wrote to his sisters: "Shall I whisper a word in your ear? The *better* people are all aristocrats. My father is too rank a Jacobin to live among them." And twenty years before Copley had been regarded by many as a Tory!

Although the boy was to make a great career in England in the law, he was unable to reclaim the farm, and its loss seemed so overwhelming to Copley that he gave up all hope of returning to America. Innumerable witnesses state that the transaction in which he got only five times his original investment remained like an open wound in his mind, embittering the rest of his life. Sixteen years later, the painter, Joseph Farington, wrote in his diary that Copley complained that the property he had sold for a few thousand pounds was now worth a hundred thousand. "Upon this he ruminates, and with other reflections founded on disappointments, passes these latter days unhappily."

Indeed, from the time of the loss of his farm Copley's star descended rapidly. In 1789, the war with France joined with the Irish rebellion to suck England into an economic depression that deepened all through the Napoleonic period. Only the most fashionable painters were able to make a living, and even their incomes were greatly reduced. Out of pity, the Prime Minister excluded artists from the war tax. Copley was not one of the most fashionable painters; after a lifetime of dreading such an eventuality, he found himself on the brink of poverty.

And now, when more than ever Copley needed his skill, a strange blight began to come over his ability to paint. As the years passed, each succeeding picture turned out less happily. Still trying to duplicate West's triumphant career, he turned to religious subjects—*Hagar and Ishmael, Abraham's Sacrifice, Saul Reproved by Samuel*—but they were not greatly admired. His new historical paintings did not succeed like the old; he was refused permission to show his *Duncan's Victory at Camperdown* in Green Park as he had shown *Gibraltar;* he had to set up his tent in a nobleman's private garden, and hardly anyone paid to see the picture.

Difficulties with engravers threw him increasingly into debt. Sharp, whom he had commissioned to make a print of *Gibraltar,* dawdled for years without even starting the plate; the subscribers demanded their money back. And when Copley commissioned a small print of *The Death of Chatham* for sale to the masses, the delivered plate was so bad he dared not publish it. He refused to pay the engraver, and the engraver sued. Bartolozzi, who had made the large print of the same subject, appeared for his colleague.

"Do you see, sir," Copley's attorney asked Bartolozzi, "in your own [print] the youngest son of Lord Chatham in a naval uniform bending forward with a tear in his eye and a countenance displaying the agony of an affectionate son on beholding a dying father; and do you see in the other an assassin, with a scar upon his cheek, exulting over the body of an old man whom he has murdered? . . . In one, the Archbishop of York appears in his true colors as a dignified and venerable prelate; in the other, his place is usurped by the drunken parson in Hogarth's *Harlot's Progress*. In one, the Earl of Chatham is supported by his son-in-law, Lord Stanhope, a figure tall, slender, and elegant; does not the other offer to view a short, sturdy porter of a bagnio, lugging home an old lecher who has got mortal drunk?"

Bartolozzi denied all this, and was followed on the stand by "an immense number of engravers" who praised the contested print. Copley's attorney then called many painters—West, Beechey, Opie, Cosway, Hoppner—who insisted Copley could not publish the print without hurting his reputation. In his charge to the jury, the judge professed total ignorance of art, and the jury ruled that Copley must pay for the engraving. Thus the artist lost nearly a thousand pounds.

Since he needed to execute some great work to revive his waning fortunes, he enthusiastically agreed to paint one of the largest conversation pieces in history; it was to show a country squire, Sir Edward Knatchbull, with his second wife and ten children. (Plate 32.) When the squire said that he missed the portrait of his first wife, Copley, in his eagerness to do something startling, suggested hanging her from the sky as one of a group of angels. Convinced that the longer he worked on a picture, the better it would be, and at best one of the slowest of painters, he mulled over every figure for months on end, until Knatchbull's youngest child, seeing him around the house so much more often than her father, made a natural mistake and called him "daddy."

After two years, the dogged painter began to near the end, but at that moment Knatchbull's second wife died. The squire married again and insisted that his third wife be put in the picture in place of the second, while the second, now also an angel, be suspended in the clouds beside the first. Copley was so eager to please that he laboriously rearranged the composition, but just as the picture again neared completion, Knatchbull appeared to say that his new wife was pregnant; a likeness of the baby, as soon as it came, must be inserted. The bewildered painter, who had put so much effort into the canvas, did not dare disagree; again much of the picture was repainted.

Working with all the relentless determination of his nature, Copley hardly allowed himself time to eat and sleep; he could not even spare a moment to write to his elder daughter, congratulating her on the birth of his first grandchild. "Sir Edward Knatchbull's picture has confined us to London," the younger daughter complained during the heat of midsummer. Life was dull while the painter slaved away interminably and no one came to call; the painter lacked time for friends. "There have been balls, masquerades, and fetes without end in honor of the peace, but I have had nothing more to do with them than reading the accounts in the papers."

Copley completed the picture after three years of toil, and sent it to the Royal Academy Exhibition of 1803. On the night of the vernissage he dressed himself in his best clothes and hurried to the gallery, anxious to savor praise and popularity once more. Sure enough, there was a crowd before his picture. Walking more firmly than he had for years, he maneuvered into position to see their faces, but then his own face grew pale. The people before him were not staring in reverence; they were smiling. Suddenly someone laughed, and at once everyone shouted with mirth; they found the two dead wives suspended from the sky irresistibly funny. When Copley tried to slink away, he felt a hand on his shoulder and saw Knatchbull himself, his face red with fury. People were mocking him, he cried; how had Copley dared show the picture without his permission? It must be removed from the show at once. Utterly discouraged, Copley nodded sadly, and the next day the hanging committee were cursing as they tried to fill with smaller pictures the space where the vast canvas had been.

But Copley's troubles with the *Knatchbull Family* were not done. The third wife now demanded that the first two be painted out; sadly the painter extended the background across the faces and figures of the angels he had so carefully delineated. The irritated baronet then refused to pay for the figures that no longer showed, insisting that Copley's charge of eighteen hundred guineas for the picture was wildly exorbitant.

When the matter was brought before a legal arbiter, Knatchbull argued that if Copley had painted the picture with decent celerity, all the changes would have been unnecessary; the third wife, the new child, would never have existed at all. He added that he had been opposed to Copley's depicting his two former wives as angels; he had wanted them shown merely as portraits hung on the wall behind him. Each side called expert witnesses. After eleven painters and engravers, including Beechey and Fuseli, had sworn that they considered Copley's charge reasonable, the arbiter decided for Copley, ignoring the testimony of the principal witness for Knatchbull: Benjamin West.

A bitter story lay behind that artist's appearance against his former protégé. When West, who had succeeded Reynolds as president of the Royal Academy, had secured through his friends an important commission which Copley had hoped to secure through his own, Copley's dislike for his benefactor rose to a ruling passion. He became a leader of the cabal that fought West in the Royal Academy, and finally forced him to resign his high office. But after a year of trying to get on without the American's leadership, the British artists re-elected him by acclaim. Copley's machinations only resulted in making him more than ever unpopular with the connoisseurs and his fellow painters.

Sitting dismally in his empty studio, he cast round for some expedient that would bring back the prosperity he had lost. As a young man he had built up his color, as he had created the rest of his technique, through hard, introspective labor. Now he undertook experiments with pigments in an attempt not so much to find tints that suited his vision as to duplicate the coloring of Titian. In 1802, his son wrote: "My father has discovered the Venetian, the true Venetian, more precious than any philosopher's stone . . . which the artists of three generations have in vain been endeavoring to explore. . . . Henceforth, then, you may fairly expect my father's pictures will transcend the productions of even Titian himself." But Copley's canvases continued to grow progressively worse. All the virtues that had made him a great artist vanished: the drawing became weak, flabby, pointless, the coloring watery, the composition empty in the extreme.

Although he had stood up against it for a long time, the pressure of Copley's English environment had been predominantly against the direction of his genius. London was a sophisticated city, and sophistication is a struggle against reality, an attempt to polish, to veneer, to hide the naked crudities of life. In its higher manifestations, it demands the use of imagination to build for man a more beautiful world; in its lower, it runs to corsets and silks and grimaces. Since Copley had been endowed neither by nature nor by his American upbringing to be a purely imaginative painter—only by using facts as a springboard could he throw himself into the air—there was real danger that, as he struggled to succeed in London, he would sink to the lower reaches of sophistication and become an artificial society artist.

Throughout his entire career, he had worked best when he had worked most realistically. In Boston, books and prints and letters from foreign-trained artists had urged him to attempt fancy pictures, but when these voices reached him from across the ocean, they had become dim and attenuated. Even the Colonial connoisseurs, who strove to think in European terms, were not quite sure what those terms were. Thus the cloak of traditional knowledge which Copley tried to throw about his shoulders was a thin garment that tore easily when he moved, revealing the naked muscles of his innate style. As his American painting grew in stature, it became increasingly literal, increasingly matter-of-fact.

Finally Copley met European art face to face. The first result of this rendezvous, his *Ascension,* showed that he possessed a dangerous skill; he was a brilliant imitator. He could have made a career out of repeating slavishly the formulas of the old masters. For a moment he tottered on the edge of the abyss; then he stepped back.

Although he had been baptized by total immersion in European art, he was too hardened a sinner to reform his homely approach overnight. And there were some aspects of his London environment that worked in favor of his genius. The centuries-old taboo against religious painting was still in force when Copley reached England. No one would pay him to enlarge his *Ascension* into a full-scale church painting. Although the style of Raphael was adored, Raphael's subject matter was forbidden. Out of the resulting confusion, Benjamin West, whose early environment had been so like Copley's, had evolved a manner which mingled the techniques of the old masters with a dry, almost scientific approach to contemporary reality. Thus Copley found waiting for him in England a prefabricated style well suited to his needs and talents.

Fortunately, the narrative pictures, which were the specialty of the Anglo-American group in London, were imaginative only in a restricted sense. Although they might arrange and heighten its elements, the painters tried to adhere to basic historical truth. Copley made his *Death of Chatham* into a collection of shrewd portraits, and in his attempt to depict the siege of Gibraltar, built models of the fortifications in his studio.

Even that fierce rendition of terror, *Brook Watson and the Shark*, is fundamentally literal-minded. Far from frightening us with imaginative symbols, Copley makes us feel that we are actual spectators of the tragedy as it occurred.

Surveying the art world of London after his arrival from America, Benjamin West had abandoned portrait painting as too social a pursuit; but Copley, who had made his reputation in that mode, persevered. His English sitters presented him with problems much more formidable than any he had faced in America. The Bostonians had, of course, wanted to be shown as finer than they were, but they wondered how lords and ladies really looked, how Reynolds would have painted them. Copley was able to take advantage of their hesitation by following his own inspiration.

The Londoners, however, had no doubts about what their social positions, real or aspired for, demanded in the likeness line. And Copley, no longer the leading painter of his world, was forced, in order to secure commissions, to make his technique agree with fashions laid down by better established artists. More dashing execution than he had ever tried in Massachusetts was demanded, brighter color, suaver backgrounds. Above all, he had to substitute for his primitive expressionism a search for the surface appearances of nature. The remodeling of his portrait style was a truly herculean labor, yet he managed to achieve a compromise between the old and the new that was in itself admirable. The bodies under the more subtly painted silk of his best English portraits remained firm, and he was still fascinated by a crudely intellectual face.

However, it was all very wearing. Copley walked perpetually on a tightrope. Beneath his feet ran the thin wire of realism that kept him elevated; to the left was the abysm of purely social painting; to the right the chasm of imaginative imitations of Raphael. As long as he remained physically strong, although he slipped and tottered sometimes, he did not fall.

At about the time that West, with the King's help, broke down the taboo against religious painting, Copley lost the thread of realism that had carried him so far. The basic reason for this catastrophe must needs escape those critics who separate an artist's life from his work. The deterioration of Copley's art was accompanied by a deterioration in his personality. He no longer had the health and strength to win a psychological battle which had to be fought over again with every picture.

Copley had always been timid and unsocial, but in Boston he had been universally respected, and he had risen to what was heroism for his character in his attempts to stop the Revolution. Although he had never felt safe in London, he had kept his apprehensions under control and functioned as a forceful and effective citizen. Now suddenly all the weaknesses and fears that had scudded through the back corridors of his mind came out of the shadows and overwhelmed him. The change was observed by diarists who scribbled down that he had become mean, cantankerous, envious, quarrelsome, vindictive. Although he lived to be seventy-seven, at sixty he showed the world all the characteristics of a broken and disgruntled old man.

The stinginess that had always been part of his character became a ruling passion. The Academy female model, Farington tells us, usually got a shilling an hour. "She is very modest in her deportment, notwithstanding her habit of exposure, and was lately married to a shoemaker. She spoke of Copley's behavior to her, who would make her sit a longer time than she could well bear to, and would scarcely pay her half-price. She had resolved not to go to him any more."

He became so crusty that it was news if he was polite to one of his fellow artists. "Copley," Farington wrote in 1807, "found me in the room alone and accosted me civilly, the first time in several years. He appeared to me to have suffered much in his faculties; his mind seemed to be incapable of comprehending what was going forward." Three years later, Farington noticed on his face a look of imbecility.

Samuel F. B. Morse, the art student who was to invent the telegraph, wrote home in 1811: "I visited Mr. Copley a few days since. He is very old and infirm. I think his age is upward of seventy, nearly the age of Mr. West. His powers of mind have almost entirely left him; his late paintings are miserable. It is really a lamentable thing that a man should outlive his faculties."

For almost twenty years Copley struggled through the twilight of old age. Always lacking money, he painted continually in an unceasing effort to produce a great picture, to secure an important commission. Occasionally he had a nervous collapse, but as soon as he was well again he picked up his brushes and returned to his studio. However, all his efforts were in vain, for the tide had set irrevocably against him. When he asked the King to pose for him, His Majesty snubbed him before the whole court. "Sit to you for a portrait! What, do you want to make a show of me?" He spent four years on an equestrian portrait of the Prince Regent that no one would purchase. When the British Institution paid three thousand guineas for West's *Christ Healing the Sick,* he set to work immediately on a vast

Resurrection, but the British Institution showed no inclination to buy it. "It makes me melancholy," wrote Mrs. Copley, "when I see his rooms so full of pictures that are highly spoken of, and I think with how much perplexity they were produced."

Copley's son had already started on the brilliant career that was to make him Lord Chancellor of England and finally Lord Lyndhurst, but for the moment his income was small, and he could contribute little to the family support. The painter was continually forced to borrow from his American son-in-law; the little letters in which he asked for one more loan are stiff with mortified pride. But even the loans that were never refused did not serve to keep up his large establishment on George Street.

After the failure of Copley's *Resurrection,* James Heath, the engraver, told Farington that Copley would have to sell everything he owned, including his house, which was already heavily mortgaged. He pointed out that Copley had become very unpopular as an artist. At about this time, Mrs. Copley wrote to her daughter: "We are, indeed, revolving what changes we can make, and whether to quit George Street. The difficulty of leaving our present situation is that it would in a great measure oblige your father to give up the pursuit of the arts; and I fear that if he should retire from them in the latter part of his life, he would feel the want of the gratification which the pursuit has accorded him."

The house was saved by a friend who took a second mortgage on it, but though his studio remained to Copley, it was no longer the refuge from the world it had been. As the painter sat before his canvas in an alien city and heard the greater rumble of the London traffic outside his window, he sometimes realized that the mistake of his life had been to leave America, to seek perfection by imitating the old masters. He scowled at the paintings of his English years that hung unsold in tiers around him, and turned to look instead at some of his American portraits which he had bought back in a vain attempt to evoke the past. He told his wife that these canvases, which he had once scorned as crude, were better than any of the highly polished works of his transatlantic career.

If only he could paint like that now! But no; he realized it was hopeless. "He sometimes says," his wife reported, "that he is too old to paint." Yet he had to paint, for in his ambitious youth he had never allowed himself time to learn to play. Work alone could distract his mind from his poverty and his frustrated career. What if the picture that grew beneath his hand was vapid and inane? It calmed his nerves to move the hand. In 1815 his wife wrote: "Your father grows feeble in his limbs; he goes very little out of the house, for walking fatigues him; but his health is good and he still pursues his profession with pleasure, and he would be uncomfortable could he not use his brush."

The tragedy had acted itself out long before the curtain fell. Still the doddering actor held the center of the stage, repeating over and over in dull parody the motions that had been the glory of his prime. He continued to paint and complain, to grow weaker and more senile, but he suffered no serious illness until his seventy-eighth year, when he was struck down during dinner by a stroke. Although it paralyzed his left side, he rallied and was able to totter around a little; even a second stroke did not kill him. His daughter wrote to her sister: "He may continue in his present state a great while, but it is so distressing that without any prospect of recovery it is not to be wished."

The old man sat stuck up in a chair like an inanimate doll, but his eyes still turned in their sockets. When he felt strong enough to talk, he told his family that he would not recover. "He was perfectly resigned and willing to die, and expressed his firm trust in God, through the merits of the Redeemer." At last God took pity. Two hours after a third stroke that left him "perfectly sensible, though unable to speak as to be understood," the long-wished-for release came. On the ninth of September, 1815, John Singleton Copley, one of the greatest painters America has ever produced, escaped at last from the long twilight of his exile.

THE END

Appendix

Bibliography

THERE EXISTS voluminous manuscript material dealing with all of Copley's life except his boyhood and youth, and almost all of it has been published. A collection concerning his American career and his trip to Italy is contained in *The Letters and Papers of John Singleton Copley and Henry Pelham, 1739-1776.* (Boston: Massachusetts Historical Society, 1904.) The originals of these documents, which seem to have come from the private files of both Copley and Pelham, were found among the papers intercepted by the British Government during the Revolution. They are in the Public Records Office, London (C.O. 5/38, 39). Although all the letters of importance were printed, in some cases there were two or three drafts of which only the most complete was used, and the editors considered a few documents so insignificant that these were omitted. Photostats of all these papers, published and unpublished, may be seen at the Massachusetts Historical Society, together with some Copley material from other collections.

A group of Copley's letters to his wife while he was in Italy, and of letters written mostly by members of his family during his English years, has been published in an abridged and edited form in Martha Babcock Amory's *The Domestic and Artistic Life of John Singleton Copley, R.A.* (Boston, 1882.) Most of these papers were recently burnt by one of Copley's descendants "because they contained allusions which she considered undesirable to preserve." A few, which came down in another branch of the family, are in the Library of Congress.

Other letters may be seen in the collections of the Boston Public

[117]

Library and the Historical Society of Pennsylvania. An important letter from Copley to Samuel Adams is in the New York Public Library.

The Copley papers are so interesting and so voluminous that it is hard to understand why no modern writer has made use of them in a biography of the great artist. Mrs. Amory's *Life* was prepared before the Copley-Pelham papers had been discovered, and in any case it is a "descendant's book," ramblingly written and given to eulogy.

Copley's American paintings have been expertly catalogued and discussed by Barbara Neville Parker and Anne Bolling Wheeler in their *John Singleton Copley, American Portraits in Oil, Pastel, and Miniature.* (Boston Museum of Fine Arts, 1938.) The last fifty pages of the book consist entirely of reproductions. I have profited from many discussions about Copley's work with the charming and erudite Mrs. Parker.

No reliable catalogue of Copley's English paintings exists; here is a labor that cries for the attention of the scholar, since our lack of an over-all survey often makes the attribution of portraits to his London period a hazardous undertaking. Even the most publicized and exhibited of such paintings, the so-called *Mrs. Seymour Fort,* raises problems. The fullest published sources of information concerning the English pictures are Augustus Thorndike Perkins's *A Sketch of the Life and a List of the Works of John Singleton Copley* (Boston, 1873); and Frank W. Bayley's *The Life and Work of John Singleton Copley, Founded on the Work of Augustus Thorndike Perkins* (Boston: Taylor Press, 1915). The biographical sections of both these books are negligible.

The most up-to-date information on Copley's American and English paintings may be found in the files of the Frick Art Reference Library, New York City. My special thanks are due to this institution for assistance and hospitality accorded to me over a period of many years. I wish to express my gratitude in particular to the director, Miss Helen Clay Frick; to Miss Ethelwyn Manning, Mrs. Hannah Johnson Howell, Miss Mildred Steinbach, and Miss Hope Mathewson.

Various other institutions and individuals have shown me great courtesies. I wish to mention in particular the staffs of the Metropolitan Museum of Art, the New York Public Library, the Museum of Fine Arts, Boston, the Worcester Art Museum, and the Yale University Art Gallery. Mr. Herbert H. Hosmer, Jr., has sent me valuable information concerning engraved sources of Copley's style.

The most interesting contemporary account of Copley will be found in William Dunlap's *History of the Rise and Progress of the Arts of Design in the United States* (2 vols., New York, 1834); or a new edition, edited by Frank W. Bayley and Charles E. Goodspeed (3 vols., Boston, Goodspeed, 1918). Dunlap copied most of his material concerning Copley's English career from Allan Cunningham's *Lives of the Most Eminent British Painters,* which is most easily available in a two-volume edition revised by Mrs. Charles Heaton and published in London during 1879.

The account of early American painting in Oskar Hagen's *The Birth of the American Tradition in Art* (New York and London, Charles Scribner's Sons, 1940), is often inaccurate and unsound. However, the chapters on Copley are the best in the book, full of brilliant analyses and only occasionally marred by faulty facts and *a-priori* reasoning.

The section on Copley in James Thomas Flexner's *America's Old Masters* (New York, The Viking Press, Inc., 1939), has been completely revised and greatly expanded to form the book you now hold in your hands.

American Painting: First Flowers of Our Wilderness, by James Thomas Flexner (Boston, Houghton Mifflin Company, 1947), discusses in detail the development of American painting during its period of rudimentary contact with European art. The book opens with the earliest known pictures created in the Colonies, and ends with Copley's departure for Europe. In the two chapters on Copley's American work, this writer has attempted to show the relationships of his canvases, not only with earlier arts and crafts, but with the social, political, and economic environment. Complete bibliographical notes on

Copley's predecessors and contemporaries—Smibert, Feke, Badger, Greenwood, Blackburn, etc.—will be found in this volume.

Other published sources of material on Copley are:

Ayer, Mary Farwell. *Boston Common in Colonial and Provincial Days.* Boston, privately printed, 1903.

Bayley, Frank W. *Five Colonial Artists of New England* (Badger, Blackburn, Copley, Feke, Smibert). Boston, privately printed, 1929.

Bolton, Theodore. *Early American Portrait Draughtsmen in Crayons.* N. Y., F. F. Sherman, 1923.

Early American Portrait Painters in Miniature. N. Y., F. F. Sherman, 1921.

Bolton, Theodore, and Binsse, Harry Lorin. "John Singleton Copley Appraised as an Artist in Relation to His Contemporaries with a Checklist of His Portraits in Oil," *Antiquarian,* XV, 1930.

Boston *Gazette.* December 2, 1773. (An account of Copley's appearance before a town meeting in connexion with the tea.)

Burroughs, Alan. *Limners and Likenesses; Three Centuries of American Painting.* Cambridge, Harvard Univ. Press, 1936.

"Young Copley," *Art in America,* XXXI, 1943.

Chamberlain, Allen. *Beacon Hill; Its Ancient Pastures and Early Mansions.* Boston, Houghton Mifflin, 1925.

Comstock, Helen. "Drawings by J. S. Copley in the Karolik Collection," *Connoisseur,* CIX, 1942.

Cunningham, C. C. "The Karolik Collection—Some Notes on Copley," *Art in America,* XXX, 1942.

Drake, Francis S. *Tea Leaves; Being a Collection of Letters and Documents Relating to the Shipment of the Tea to the American Colonies in the Year 1773.* Boston, 1884.

Einstein, Lewis. *Divided Loyalties; Americans in England during the War of Independence.* Boston, Houghton Mifflin, 1933.

Farington, Joseph. *The Farington Diary, Edited by James Grieg.* 8

vols., N. Y., Doubleday, Page, 1922-29; London, Hutchinson, 1922-27.

Foote, Henry Wilder. "When was John Singleton Copley Born?" *New England Quarterly*, X, 1937.

Graves, Algernon. *Royal Academy of Arts; a Complete Dictionary of the Contributors and Their Work from Its Foundation in 1769 to 1904.* 8 vols., London, Henry Graves, 1905-06.

The Society of Artists of Great Britain, 1760-1791; the Free Society of Artists, 1761-1783; a Complete Dictionary of Contributors and Their Works. London, Bell and Graves, 1907.

Healy, G. P. A. "Reminiscences of a Portrait Painter," *North Am. Review*, CLI, 1890.

Hutchinson, Thomas. *The Diary and Letters of His Excellency Thomas Hutchinson, compiled by Peter Orlando Hutchinson.* 2 vols., Boston, 1886.

Isham, Samuel. *The History of American Painting.* N. Y., Macmillan, 1916.

Jeffrey, Margaret. "A Painting of Copley's English Period [Brook Watson and the Shark]," *Metropolitan Museum Bulletin*, I, 1942.

La Follette, Suzanne. *Art in America.* N. Y., Harper, 1929.

Lee, Cuthbert. *Early American Portrait Painters.* (With discussions of pictures in public collections.) New Haven, Yale Univ. Press, 1929.

Masters in Art: Copley. Boston, Bates and Guild, 1904.

Metropolitan Museum of Art. *Catalogue of Copley Exhibition.* N. Y., 1936.

Miller, John Chester. *Sam Adams; Pioneer in Propaganda.* Boston, Little, Brown, 1936.

Morgan, John Hill. "Some Notes on John Singleton Copley," *Antiques*, XXXI, 1937.

John Singleton Copley, 1737/8-1815. Windham, Conn., 1939.

[122]

Morison, Samuel Eliot. "The Commerce of Boston on the Eve of the Revolution," *Proc. Am. Antiquarian Assoc.*, XXXII, Worcester, 1922.

Monkhouse, William Cosmo. *Masterpieces of English Art.* London, 1869.

Morse, Edward Lind. *Samuel F. B. Morse, His Letters and Journals.* 2 vols., Boston, Houghton Mifflin, 1914.

Parker, Barbara Neville. "Problems of Attribution in Early Portraits by Copley," *Bulletin of the Museum of Fine Arts, Boston*, XL, 1942.

Rankin, William. "An Impression of the Early Works of John Singleton Copley," *Burlington Magazine*, VIII, 1905.

Richardson, E. P. "Watson and the Shark by John Singleton Copley," *Art Quarterly*, X, 1947.

Sherman, Frederick Fairchild. "Portraits and Miniatures by Copley," *Art in America*, XVI, 1928.

"John Singleton Copley as a Portrait Miniaturist," *Art in America*, XVIII, 1930.

Sitwell, Osbert. *Left Hand, Right Hand.* Boston, Little Brown, 1944.

Sitwell, Sacheverell. *Conversation Pieces.* N. Y., Scribner; and London, Batsford, 1937.

Slade, D. R. "Henry Pelham, the Half-Brother of John Singleton Copley," *Publications of the Colonial Soc. of Mass.*, V, Boston, 1902.

Spielmann, Marion Henry. *British Portrait Painting to the Opening of the Nineteenth Century.* Vol. 2. London, Berlin Photographic Co., 1910.

Stark, James H. *The Loyalists of Massachusetts.* Boston, W. B. Clarke, 1907.

Tuckerman, Henry Theodore. *Book of the Artists.* N. Y., 1867.

Walker, John, and James Macgill. *Great American Painting from Smibert to Bellows.* N. Y., Oxford Univ. Press, 1943.

Watson, Elkanah. *Men and Times of the Revolution, or the Memoirs of Watson.* N. Y., 1856.

Wehle, H. B. *American Miniatures, 1730-1850* (with a biographical dictionary of the artists by Theodore Bolton). Garden City, Doubleday, Page, 1927.

West, Benjamin. *A Discourse to the Students of the Royal Academy, December 10, 1792.* London, 1792.

Whitley, William T. *Artists and Their Friends in England, 1700-1799.* 2 vols., London, Medici Society, 1928.

Art in England, 1800-1820. Cambridge Univ. Press, 1928.

Whitmore, William H. "The Early Painters and Engravers of New England," *Proc. Mass. Hist. Soc.,* IX, 1866-67.

"Notes Concerning Peter Pelham, the Earliest Artist Resident in New England, and His Successors Prior to the Revolution," *Proc. Mass. Hist. Soc.,* IX, 1866-67.

Wind, Edgar. "The Revolution of History Painting," *Journal of the Warburg Institute,* II, 1938.

Books published since 1948:

Klayman, Richard. *America Abandoned: John Singleton Copley's American Years, 1738–1774, an Interpretive History.* New York, University Press of America, 1983.

Prown, Jules David. *John Singleton Copley.* Volume I: America; Volume II: England. Cambridge, Harvard University Press, 1966. Published for the National Gallery of Art, Washington. (Particularly important for the checklist of Copley's English paintings.)

Illustrations

JOHN SINGLETON COPLEY: *Boy with Squirrel*   *Museum of Fine Arts, Boston*

Plate 1

JOHN SINGLETON COPLEY: *Mrs. Benjamin Pickman*   *Yale University*

Plate 2

JOHN SINGLETON COPLEY: *Benjamin Pickman*   *Yale University*

Plate 3

JOHN SINGLETON COPLEY: *Governor and Mrs. Thomas Mifflin*   *The Historical Society of Pennsylvania*

Plate 4

JOHN SINGLETON COPLEY: *James Otis*

Wichita Art Museum

Plate 5

JOHN SINGLETON COPLEY: *The Death of Major Pierson*

Tate Gallery, London

Plate 6

JOHN SINGLETON COPLEY: *The Death of Chatham*

Plate 7

JOHN SINGLETON COPLEY: *Brook Watson and the Shark*

Plate 8

JOHN SINGLETON COPLEY: *Self-Portrait in Pastel*   *Winterthur Museum*

Plate 9

PETER PELHAM: *Reverend Cotton Mather*
American Antiquarian Society

JOSEPH BADGER: *Reverend Jonathan Edwards, Senior*
Yale University

ROBERT FEKE: *Mrs. James Bowdoin*
Bowdoin Museum of Fine Arts

JOHN GREENWOOD: *Mrs. Francis Cabot*
Bertram K. and Nina Fletcher Little Collection

EARLY SOURCES OF COPLEY'S STYLE

Plate 10

JOHN SINGLETON COPLEY: *Ann Tyng*
Museum of Fine Arts, Boston

JOSEPH BLACKBURN: *Mary Sylvester Dering*
Owned anonymously

JOHN SINGLETON COPLEY: *Elizabeth Ross*
Museum of Fine Arts, Boston

SIR JOSHUA REYNOLDS: *The Ladies Amabel and*
Mary Jemima Yorke *Cleveland Museum of Art*

LATER SOURCES OF COPLEY'S STYLE

Plate 11

JOHN SINGLETON COPLEY: *The Brother and Sisters of Christopher Gore* *Winterthur Museum*

JOHN SINGLETON COPLEY: *Battle Scene* *Addison Gallery of American Art, Andover, Massachusetts*

Plate 12

JOHN SINGLETON COPLEY: *Mrs. Joseph Mann*

Museum of Fine Arts, Boston

Plate 13

Self-Portrait
Museum of Fine Arts, Boston

Deborah Scollay
Worcester Art Museum

Nathaniel Hurd
Owned anonymously

Samuel Cary
Owned anonymously

Mrs. Samuel Cary
Owned anonymously

Plate 14   COPLEY MINIATURES

JOHN SINGLETON COPLEY: *William Brattle*

Harvard University

Plate 15

JOHN SINGLETON COPLEY: *Epes Sargent, Senior*   *National Gallery of Art, Washington*

Plate 16

Jоhn Singleton Copley: *Detail of Epes Sargent, Senior*

Plate 17

JOHN SINGLETON COPLEY: *Mrs. Nathaniel Appleton*

Harvard University

Plate 18

JOHN SINGLETON COPLEY: *Mary Warner*   *Toledo Museum of Art*

Plate 19

JOHN SINGLETON COPLEY: *Mrs. Paul Richard*   *Museum of Fine Arts, Houston*

Plate 20

JOHN SINGLETON COPLEY: *Thomas Amory II*　　　　　　　　　　　　　　*Corcoran Gallery*

Plate 21

JOHN SINGLETON COPLEY: *Mrs. Ezekial Goldthwait*   *Museum of Fine Arts, Boston*

Plate 22

JOHN SINGLETON COPLEY: *Thomas Hancock*   *Harvard University*

Plate 23

JOHN SINGLETON COPLEY: *Professor John Winthrop*

Harvard University

Plate 24

JOHN SINGLETON COPLEY: *The Ascension*

Museum of Fine Arts, Boston

Plate 25

JOHN SINGLETON COPLEY: *Drawings for The Death of Major Pierson*   *Owned anonymously*

Plate 26

JOHN SINGLETON COPLEY: *Colonels Hugo and Schleppengull*   *Fogg Art Museum, Harvard University*

Plate 27

JOHN SINGLETON COPLEY: *Midshipman Augustus Brine*

Plate 28

JOHN SINGLETON COPLEY: *Henry Addington, First Viscount Sidmouth*   *The Saint Louis Art Museum*

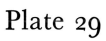

Plate 29

JOHN SINGLETON COPLEY: *Mr. and Mrs. Ralph Izard*

Plate 30

JOHN SINGLETON COPLEY: *The Copley Family*

Plate 31

JOHN SINGLETON COPLEY: *Sketch for the Knatchbull Family*

Plate 32

Catalogue of Illustrations

All dimensions are given in inches, the height before the width.

BADGER, JOSEPH: *Reverend Jonathan Edwards, Senior*; oil on canvas; 30 × 25½; c. 1750–1755; Yale University Art Gallery; bequest of Eugene Phelps Edwards. Plate 10.

BLACKBURN, JOSEPH: *Mrs. Thomas Dering (Mary Sylvester)*; oil on canvas; 49⅞ × 40⅛; owned anonymously. Plate 11.

COPLEY, JOHN SINGLETON:
Henry Addington, 1st Viscount Sidmouth; 93½ × 64; 1797–1798; The Saint Louis Art Museum; museum purchase. Plate 29.
Thomas Amory II; oil on canvas; 49½ × 39¾; c. 1770–c. 1774; in the collection of The Corcoran Gallery of Art, museum purchase. Plate 21.
Mrs. Nathaniel Appleton (Margaret Gibbs); oil on canvas; 35⁵/₁₆ × 29¹/₁₆ (the picture has probably been cut down from a three-quarter length); 1763; courtesy of the Harvard University Portrait Collection, Harvard University Art Museums; left in the keeping of Harvard College by John James Appleton, March 19, 1855. Plate 18.
The Ascension; oil on canvas; 32 × 29; 1775; bequest of Susan Greene Dexter in memory of Charles and Martha Babcock Amory; courtesy, Museum of Fine Arts, Boston. Plate 25.

Boy with Squirrel (*Henry Pelham*); oil on canvas; 30¼ × 25; c. 1765; gift of the artist's great granddaughter; courtesy of the Museum of Fine Arts, Boston.   Plate 1.

William Brattle; oil on canvas; 49½ × 39¾; 1756; courtesy of the Fogg Art Museum, Harvard University Art Museums. Gift in part—Mrs. Thomas Brattle Gannett. Purchase in part through funds from Robert T. Gannett, an anonymous donor, and the Alpheus Hyatt Fund.   Plate 15.

Midshipman Augustus Brine; oil on canvas; 50 × 40; 1782; bequest of Richard Wolfe Brixley, 1943 (43.86.4), Metropolitan Museum of Art.   Plate 28.

Samuel Cary; watercolor on ivory; oval, 1⅜ × 1¼; owned anonymously.   Plate 14.

Mrs. Samuel Cary (*Sarah Gray*); watercolor on ivory; oval, 1⅜ × 1¼; owned anonymously.   Plate 14.

The Copley Family; oil on canvas, 72½ × 90¼; framed 89 × 107 × 5½; 1776/1777; Andrew W. Mellon Fund. © 1993 National Gallery of Art, Washington, D.C.   Plate 31.

Self Portrait; watercolor on porcelain; oval 1⅝ × 1¼; Gift of Copley Amory; Courtesy, Museum of Fine Arts, Boston.   Plate 14.

Self Portrait; pastel on paper; c. 23 × c. 17; c. 1770; Courtesy, Winterthur Museum, Winterthur, Delaware.   Plate 1.

Death of the Earl of Chatham; oil on canvas; 89 × 120; 1779–1780; The Tate Gallery, London.   Plate 7.

Death of Major Pierson; oil on canvas, 99 × 144; 1783. In the *Dictionary of National Biography* the Major's name is spelt "Peirson," but the National Gallery uses the spelling here given. [The Tate Gallery uses the spelling "Pearson."] The Tate Gallery, London.
                                                      Plate 6.

Death of Major Pierson, drawings for the picture; Studies of the figures of fleeing woman and child, and of boy in hat; pencil, black and white chalk on gray-blue paper; 13⅞ × 22¼; c. 1783; owned anonymously.   Plate 26.

Studies of officers with Major Pierson, and of fleeing woman and child;
black and white chalk on gray-blue paper; 13¾ × 22¼; c. 1783;
owned anonymously.   Plate 26.

Mrs. Ezekiel Goldthwait (Elizabeth Lewis); oil on canvas; 50 × 40; c.
1771; bequest of John T. Bowen in memory of Eliza M. Bowen;
courtesy, Museum of Fine Arts, Boston.

Brother and Sisters of Christopher Gore; oil on canvas; 40½ × 56¼; c.
1753; courtesy, Winterthur Museum, Winterthur, Delaware.
                                                      Plate 12.

Thomas Hancock; oil on canvas; 95½ × 59½; c. 1764–1766; courtesy of the Harvard University Portrait Collection, Harvard University Art Museums; given by John Hancock, nephew of
Thomas Hancock, to Harvard College, 1766.   Plate 23.

*Colonels Hugo and Schleppengull; sketch made in Germany for Copley's
"Repulse of the Floating Batteries at Gibraltar"*; oil on canvas; 25¾
× 21¾; 1787; courtesy of the Fogg Art Museum, Harvard University Art Museums; gift of Mrs. Gordon Dexter.   Plate 27.

Nathaniel Hurd; miniature on copper; 2¾ × 2⅛; owned anonymously.   Plate 14.

Mr. and Mrs. Ralph Izard (Alice Delancey); oil on canvas; 69 × 88½;
1775; Edward Ingersoll Browne Fund; courtesy, Museum of
Fine Arts, Boston.   Plate 30.

The Family of Sir Edward Knatchbull (sketch for the large picture); oil on
canvas; 25½ × 37½; late English period; The Knatchbull Portrait Collection; Photograph, Courtauld Institute of Art.
                                                      Plate 32.

Mrs. Joseph Mann (Bethia Torrey); oil on canvas; 36½ × 28¼; 1753;
gift of Frederick and Holbrook E. Metcalf; courtesy, Museum of
Fine Arts, Boston.   Plate 13.

Thomas Mifflin and Mrs. Sarah (Morris) Mifflin; oil on canvas; 60½
× 48; 1773; courtesy of The Historical Society of Pennsylvania
(1900.2).   Plate 4.

James Otis; oil on canvas; 49½ × 39½; c. 1760; The Roland P. Murdock Collection, Wichita Art Museum, Wichita, Kansas.

Plate 5.

Henry Pelham; see *Boy with Squirrel.*

Benjamin Pickman; oil on canvas; 50⅜ × 40¼; c. 1758–1761; Yale University Art Gallery; bequest of Edith Malvina K. Wetmore.

Plate 2.

Mrs. Benjamin Pickman (Mary Toppan); oil on canvas; 50 × 40; 1763; Yale University Art Gallery; bequest of Edith Malvina K. Wetmore.

Plate 3.

Mrs. Paul Richard (Elizabeth Garland); oil on canvas; 49 × 39; c. 1771. Museum of Fine Arts, Houston: The Bayou Bend Collection; gift of Miss Ima Hogg.

Plate 20.

Elizabeth Ross (Mrs. William Tyng); oil on canvas; 50 × 40; c. 1767; M. and M. Karolik Collection of Eighteenth Century American Arts; courtesy, Museum of Fine Arts, Boston.

Plate 11.

Epes Sargent, Senior; oil on canvas; 49⅞ × 40; framed 57 × 46½; c. 1760; gift of the Avalon foundation, © 1993 National Gallery of Art, Washington, D.C.

Plates 16 and 17.

Deborah Scollay (Mrs. John Melville); watercolor on ivory; oval 1 × ⅞; c. 1762; courtesy of the Worcester Art Museum, Worcester, Massachusetts.

Plate 14.

The Three Youngest Daughters of George III; oil on canvas; 20½ × 15½; The Royal Collection © 1993 Her Majesty Queen Elizabeth II.

Frontispiece

Battle Scene; ink on laid paper, 3⅝ × 7; 1754; © Addison Gallery of American Art, Phillips Academy, Andover, Massachusetts. All Rights Reserved.

Plate 12.

Ann Tyng (Mrs. Thomas Smelt); oil on canvas; 50 × 40¼; 1756; Juliana Cheney Edwards Collection; courtesy, Museum of Fine Arts, Boston.

Plate 11.

Mary Warner (Mrs. Samuel Sherburne); *Young Lady with a Bird and Dog*; oil on canvas; 48 × 40; 1767; The Toledo Museum of Art; purchased with funds from the Florence Scott Libbey Bequest in Memory of her Father, Maurice A. Scott.   Plate 19.

Brook Watson and the Shark (one of several versions of this picture); oil on canvas; 72⅛ × 90¼; 1778; gift of Mrs. George von Lengerke Myer; courtesy, Museum of Fine Arts, Boston.   Plate 8.

Professor John Winthrop; oil on canvas; 50¼ × 40 14; c. 1770–c. 1774; courtesy of the Harvard University Portrait Collection, Harvard University Art Museums; gift of the estate of John Winthrop, his grandson, 1894.   Plate 24.

FEKE, ROBERT: *Mrs. James Bowdoin II (Elizabeth Erving)*; oil on canvas; 50⅛ × 40⅛; 1748; Bowdoin College Museum of Art, Brunswick, Maine; bequest of Sarah Bowdoin Dearborn.   Plate 10.

GREENWOOD, JOHN: *Mrs. Francis Cabot (Mary Fitch)*; oil on canvas; 36 × 28⅛; Bertram K. and Nina Fletcher Little Collection; courtesy of John B. Little, M.D.   Plate 10.

PELHAM, PETER: *Reverend Cotton Mather*; oil on canvas; 30 × 25; c. 1727; courtesy, American Antiquarian Society.   Plate 10.

REYNOLDS, SIR JOSHUA: *The Ladies Amabel and Mary Jemima Yorke*; oil on canvas; 1760; 77 × 67; Joshua Reynolds; British; 1723–1792; © The Cleveland Museum of Art, bequest of John L. Severance, 42.645. This portrait was engraved in its entirety several times during the early 1760s. In addition, Valentine Green published in 1763 a print, entitled *Miss Watson,* which showed only the figure of the older girl. One of these engravings was undoubtedly the source for Copley's *Elizabeth Ross.*   Plate 10.

Index

Index